Leadership That Fits Your Church

What Kind of Pastor for What Kind of Congregation

Leadership That Fits Your Church

What Kind of Pastor for What Kind of Congregation

Cynthia Woolever
& Deborah Bruce

CHALICE
PRESS

ST. LOUIS, MISSOURI

Bible quotations, unless otherwise noted, are from the *New Revised Standard Version Bible*, copyright 1989, Division of Christian Education of the National Council of the Churches of Christ in the United States of America. Used by permission. All rights reserved.

The U.S. Congregational Life Survey was conducted in compliance with the American Association for Public Opinion Research's (AAPOR) Code of Professional Ethics and Practices, which may be found on the AAPOR Web site at http://www.aapor.org/ethics.

Cover and interior design: Scribe Inc.

Cartoons: © Chris Morgan, http://www.exmedia.com.

www.chalicepress.com

10 9 8 7 6 5 4 3 2 1   12 13 14 15 16 17

PRINT: 9780827221734   EPUB: 9780827221741   EPDF: 9780827221758

Library of Congress Cataloging-in-Publication Data

Woolever, Cynthia.
  Leadership that fits your church: what kind of pastor for what kind of
    congregation : / Cynthia Woolever and Deborah Bruce.
      p. cm.
  ISBN 978-0-8272-2173-4
  1. Pastoral theology. 2. Christian leadership. I. Bruce, Deborah. II. Title.
  BV4011.3.W67 2012
  253–dc23

*In memory of collaborator and friend Deborah Bruce (1955 – 2012),
who graced my life for sixteen years with her intelligence
and sense of humor.*

Contents

Editor's Foreword

Inspiration and Wisdom for Twenty-First-Century Christian Leaders

You have chosen wisely in deciding to study and learn from a book published in **The Columbia Partnership Leadership Series** with Chalice Press. We publish for

- Congregational leaders who desire to serve with greater faithfulness, effectiveness, and innovation.
- Christian ministers who seek to pursue and sustain excellence in ministry service.
- Members of congregations who desire to reach their full kingdom potential.
- Christian leaders who desire to use a coach approach in their ministry.
- Denominational and parachurch leaders who want to come alongside affiliated congregations in a servant leadership role.
- Consultants and coaches who desire to increase their learning concerning the congregations and Christian leaders they serve.

The Columbia Partnership Leadership Series is an inspiration- and wisdom-sharing vehicle of The Columbia Partnership, a community of Christian leaders who are seeking to transform the capacity of the North American church to pursue and sustain vital Christ-centered ministry. You can connect with us at www.TheColumbiaPartnership.org.

Primarily serving congregations, denominations, educational institutions, leadership development programs, and parachurch organizations, the Partnership also seeks to connect with individuals, businesses, and other organizations seeking a Christ-centered spiritual focus.

We welcome your comments on these books, and we welcome your suggestions for new subject areas and authors we ought to consider.

George W. Bullard Jr., Senior Editor
GBullard@TheColumbiaPartnership.org

The Columbia Partnership,
332 Valley Springs Road, Columbia, SC 29223-6934
Voice: 803.622.0923, www.TheColumbiaPartnership.org

Acknowledgments

We give special thanks . . .

To Katie Duncan, Hilary Harris, Joelle Kopacz, and Ida Smith-Williams, whose hard work, diligence, enthusiasm, and good humor helped us accomplish all that was needed for this huge project.

To everyone else in Research Services, Presbyterian Church (USA), who contributed in countless ways to make this project happen: Jack Marcum (coordinator), Perry Chang, Susan King, Becki Moody, Jonathan Moody, Gail Quets, and Christy Riggs.

To those at Harris Interactive, Inc., who identified the random sample of congregations, invited them to participate in the survey, and made extra efforts to obtain input from the key leader in each congregation.

To colleagues who gave guidance and shared insights: Kevin Armstrong, Steve Boots, Mark Chaves, Ann Deibert, Robert Dixon, Stephen Fichter, Leslie Francis, Mary Gautier, Kirk Hadaway, Trey Hammond, Dale Jones, Leslie King, Penny Marler, Herb Miller, Sharon Miller, Marcia Myers, Mandy Robbins, David Roozen, Chris Schroeder, Cass Shaw, and Scott Thumma.

To colleagues who helped lead the way during Wave 1: Jackson Carroll, Becky McMillan Haney, Matthew Price, and Keith Wulff.

To research colleagues who directed the denominational oversamples for Wave 2: James Bowers, Laura Chambers, Roger Dudley, Rich Houseal, Destiny Hisey, Marty Smith, and Richie Stanley.

To international colleagues with whom we collaborated on the International Congregational Life Survey and whose earlier work set the stage for this project: John Bellamy, Keith Castle, Howard Dillon, Robert Dixon, Dean Drayton, Peter Kaldor, Ruth Powell, Tina Rendell, and Sam Sterling (Australia); Norman Brookes (New Zealand); and Phillip Escott, Alison Gelder, and Roger Whitehead (United Kingdom).

To those at Chalice Press who helped bring this book to fruition: George Bullard, Trent Butler, Brad Lyons, and Gail Stobaugh.

To our funding organizations and their officers: Chris Coble and John Wimmer of Lilly Endowment Inc. and James Lewis of the Louisville Institute.

And, most important, to the many pastors, priests, rabbis, and other key leaders who gave their time to participate in the U.S. Congregational Life Survey, telling us about their joys and challenges in ministry. Together with the responses of worshipers in their congregations, we based this book on their generous contributions.

Preface

The pastor and people in the pew carry out church ministries as partners. We designed this book to give insights to pastors and lay leadership who want to strengthen (a) their personal sense of meaning and satisfaction in ministry and (b) the effectiveness of their congregation's ministry.

Who Should Read This Book?

This book is for pastors. Our research points to the kinds of pastoral leaders that effectively serve a range of congregational types. We wish to encourage pastors and other leadership staff to assess their strengths for ministry and understand the church contexts where those talents might best fit. This book can assist pastors in recognizing sources of satisfaction and stress in ministry.

This book is for lay leadership and members. Pastoral leaders are as diverse as sunsets. What kind of pastor might be the best fit for the congregation? When leaders and members know more about what pastors experience, they can discover ways that they, as a congregation, can support their pastor. And they can better collaborate with the pastor to enhance congregational effectiveness.

This book is for denominational leaders, church consultants, seminary faculty and students, and academics. Professionals who help congregations move forward, equip congregational leaders, and mentor or coach pastors can develop an eye for pastoral leadership that is the "best fit" for a specific congregational context. Our findings illustrate critical leadership factors that foster organizational effectiveness and mission achievement in congregations.

How Is This Portrait of Pastoral Leadership Different from Other Clergy Profiles?

The chapters that follow offer a view of American pastoral leadership that is distinct from other descriptions:

- *A large representative national sample of pastoral leaders, congregations, and parishes participated in the study.* Many previous studies of clergy and congregational life derive from small samples or in-depth case studies.[1] Because the pastors and congregations involved in these previous studies may not be typical, the results were not representative of or applicable to all pastors or congregations. Pastors and worshipers in a wide variety of congregations participated in the U.S. Congregational

Life Survey: from every state across the country; from rural, suburban, and urban areas; and from both growing communities and communities in decline.

- *A broad range of denominations and faith groups took part.* Consultants
and other experts on congregational life give advice based on years
of experience working with congregations. However, observations by
such experts are often limited to the range of pastors and congregations they encounter in their work. Our scientific research based on
a random sample of U.S. congregations supplements these perspectives by showing a current snapshot of pastors in the context of their
congregations. This research provides an opportunity to test our own
theories and the recommendations of denominational leaders and
consultants.
- *The experiences of pastors in congregations of all sizes are included.* Too often
researchers and congregational consultants select large congregations
or megachurches, rapidly growing congregations, congregations with
one-of-a-kind ministries, congregations in conflict, or congregations
and parishes that are unique in some other way. This causes difficulties for leaders and attendees who attempt to apply the lessons in
small or midsized congregations, declining or stable communities, or
other settings. Our findings complement and expand research on pastoral leadership found elsewhere.[2]
- *We asked the opinions of both pastoral leaders and worshipers in the same
congregation.* This distinction is vital. Most previous studies relied on
the views and opinions of clergy or a single lay leader in each congregation. The U.S. Congregational Life Survey records the views of half
a million people who regularly invest in congregational life through
their participation in worship. Together with information from pastoral leaders and clergy, their *combined* responses are the definitive
source of information about pastoral leadership in the context of the
congregation.

The U.S. Congregational Life Survey

Our examination of pastoral ministry relies on findings from the U.S.
Congregational Life Survey. Funded by generous grants from Lilly Endowment, Inc. and the Louisville Institute, the U.S. Congregational Life Survey
provides the largest and most representative profile of worshipers and
their congregations ever developed in the United States. More than half
a million worshipers in 500,000 have participated by filling out a survey
during religious services.

The U.S. Congregational Life Survey project comprises several layers
of information. In addition to surveys completed by worshipers, we also
asked one key pastoral leader in each participating congregation to respond
to a survey about their ministry tasks, job satisfaction, sources of support

and stress, compensation, and theological education. Responses from 692 leaders who took part in the survey in 2008 and 2009 form the basis for this book. Our goal here is to describe pastoral leaders—those pastors, priests, and other leaders who serve in local congregations—*and* the church contexts where they serve. (Appendix 1 details our survey methodology.)

Our look at pastoral leaders and their congregations reflects our understanding of church vitality. In *Beyond the Ordinary: Ten Strengths of U.S. Congregations,* we detailed ten aspects of church life that are important for successful congregations.[3] Strong congregations (1) help their worshipers grow spiritually, (2) provide meaningful worship, (3) are places where worshipers participate in the congregation in many ways, (4) give worshipers a sense of belonging, (5) care for children and youth, (6) focus on the community, (7) help worshipers share their faith with others, (8) welcome new people, (9) rely on empowering congregational leadership, and (10) have a positive outlook on the future. Although we found that all congregations have strengths, no congregation exhibits *all* the strengths we identified. Individual congregations reveal and build on their strengths in unique ways. (Appendix 2 explains how any congregation can take part in the U.S. Congregational Life Survey to understand their worshipers and identify strengths.)

Why Us?

We share with The Columbia Partnership (TCP) Leadership Series and Chalice Press the desire to help congregations become more effective in their ministries. We also share the same audience—those people and organizations that provide leadership and support for congregational ministry. And we believe that an essential part of good decision making by congregational leaders involves accurate information about how churches work, which results from the U.S. Congregational Life Survey provide.

One of us (Cynthia) has a doctorate in sociology. As a practitioner of religious organizational research, Cynthia has 25 years of experience working with congregations, judicatories, and seminaries. She is currently the lead researcher for the U.S. Congregational Life Survey and coeditor of *The Parish Paper* with Lyle Schaller and Herb Miller.

The other one of us (Deborah) is a psychologist with experience in a variety of applied research settings. Deborah has served the Presbyterian Church (USA) as manager of the Research Services office for 19 years and is also project manager of the U.S. Congregational Life Survey. She has made numerous presentations to denominational and judicatory leaders about congregational life, evangelism, and church growth.

Together we have written three books for pastors and lay leaders aimed at strengthening congregations: *A Field Guide to U.S. Congregations, Beyond the Ordinary: Ten Strengths of U.S. Congregations,* and *Places of Promise: Finding Strength in Your Congregation's Location.* We regularly blog and tweet our most recent findings about church life.[4]

Why This Book Now?

In this book we turn our attention to effective pastoral leadership. This topic remains important because the task of leading congregations has never been more daunting. The current financial climate coupled with community changes, increasing operating costs, rising lay expectations, and the decreasing role of religion in society result in challenges for even the most talented pastor.

What is different about this book? First, many books on pastoral leadership are written exclusively for the pastor and/or from the pastor's point of view. Lay leaders seldom read about the critical part they play in directing the church's future. This book presents a 360-degree data-driven view of all that is involved in congregational vitality: the values, commitments, experiences, and perceptions of members, lay leaders, and pastors.

Second, other books about pastoral leadership focus on broad concepts like vision casting or negotiating change. Although these books can be helpful to clergy, the texts rarely share much information that would help average church members better understand what kind of pastor might be the best fit for their congregation, nor do these volumes mention how to support their pastor effectively.

Third, though another relevant set of volumes includes excellent reviews of leadership in changing organizations (see books by Ronald Heifetz, Stewart Friedman, John Kotter, and Edgar Schein), the authors of such books are not writing exclusively for congregations or religious audiences. Many lay leaders and pastors would find translating the content of such books to the particulars of church life to be demanding.

Our efforts draw a comprehensive picture of America's pastoral leadership in the context of the local congregation. The chapters progress from basic descriptions of pastors and church types to illustrations of the more complex dynamics that yield a good match between congregational features and pastoral leadership. Chapter 1 sets the stage by highlighting several significant trends that make pastoral leadership difficult. Then, we describe the variety of pastoral leaders serving in churches today: their profiles by age, gender, education, ministry tasks, and years of experience (Chapter 2). Next, we depict the kinds of congregations where pastors serve (Chapter 3). In Chapters 4 and 5, we explore sources of support and stress in relationship to the pastoral profiles outlined in Chapter 2. What gives pastors the greatest satisfaction in their ministry? What experiences or ministry tasks generate stress or hardship? In Chapter 6, we search for the implications of pastoral satisfaction and well-being. What do congregations risk if their pastor is not satisfied or if his or her job stress becomes unmanageable? Chapter 7 investigates a particular type of congregation—numerically growing congregations—and the leadership patterns associated with that growth. Chapter 8 explores pastoral effectiveness in a broader sense. Are some leadership styles or skills linked to congregational strength in worship or high levels of worshiper participation? We pursue pastoral leadership approaches in Chapter 9. Finally, Chapter 10 focuses on the key question of this book: what makes for a good match between a pastoral leader and a congregation?

We follow the pastoral transition experiences of three churches: mainline Protestant Franklin Downtown Church, conservative Protestant Pines Community Church, and a Catholic parish, St. Mary's. The stories of these pastors and churches shine light on the complexity of change. In Chapter 10, we summarize what other congregations can learn from their missteps and successes.

Our ultimate goal is to help pastors see themselves and their ministry more clearly. We hope to convey the sources of pastoral satisfaction as well as the sources of stress in pastoral ministry that are obstacles to clergy. We believe a greater understanding of clergy will help lay leaders involved in pastoral searches discern the type of clergyperson that best fits the needs and values of their congregation. Ideally, this book will also inspire lay leaders to recognize their ministry gifts and the critical partnership role they play in the congregation's overall vitality.

Chapter 1

What Kind of Pastor for
What Kind of Congregation?

Three churches face a common situation: a pastoral transition. Their efforts to find a pastor who is a good match for the congregation or to improve the pastor-church fit will illustrate each chapter's main ideas. Their stories also underscore the high stakes for lay leaders and pastors who want only the best for their congregation's ministries. Our first case study involves a mainline Protestant church.[1]

Franklin Downtown Church

After serving faithfully for 17 years, the congregation's much-loved pastor retired. An interim pastor began helping the church prepare for a new pastor. The lay leaders formed a search committee that represented the congregation's diversity: newcomers, young people, seniors, and parents. The search committee used an every-member survey to identify the skills and traits they wanted in their next pastor. The interim pastor challenged them to think about not only what current members wanted but also the kind of pastor the church needed in the future. The committee decided they would seriously consider calling someone who met seven of their ten most-desired pastoral traits. Using these criteria, they selected from more than 50 pastors who were interested in the call.

Chris was one of the pastors who caught their attention. After serving six years as an associate pastor in another state, he and his wife sensed that it was time to consider a move. Chris felt called to be a solo pastor and saw his associate pastor experience as good preparation. Franklin Downtown Church seemed to be a theologically moderate and healthy congregation that offered all that they had hoped for in a new call. Located in Chris's home state, the church would make it possible to be closer to family, a plus given their young children. The church's location was desirable for other reasons, too; it was in a college community with many professionals and cultural events. Finally, as a financially secure church, it offered a good salary.

As the search committee begins interviewing pastors, will they be able to hold to the skills and traits they committed to in the beginning? Or as they interview potential candidates face to face, will they be willing to modify that list if a candidate interviews well and captures their hearts? What do Chris and the committee need to know to determine if this congregation is a good fit for his leadership gifts?

Why Effective Congregational Leadership Is More Difficult than Ever

Social change over the past four decades continues to alter the landscape for pastoral ministry and congregations. Here we outline a few significant trends that influence all pastoral transitions.[2]

More member mobility. Between 40 and 70% of worshipers in a typical congregation grew up in or transferred their membership from a congregation in another denomination.[3] People in different denominations vary in their definitions of good leadership and effective congregational ministry, so these switchers bring numerous expectations to their new congregations. Pastors lead churches whose members, having arrived from diverse faith traditions, want to go in several directions simultaneously.

Many churches encounter high turnover in the pews. One in three worshipers in the typical congregation is *new*–attending his or her current congregation for five years or less. In Protestant churches, the largest group of *new* worshipers is *switchers* (38%).[4] Switchers are prompted to change denominations by marriage to someone of another faith, moving to a new community, changes in their values and preferences, and other reasons. Another third of *new* worshipers are either *first-timers* (9%)–people who have never regularly attended anywhere–or *returnees* (22%)–people who attended religious services earlier in their lives and now are returning to participation. *Transfers*, who make up the final third of *new* worshipers (31%), come from another church within the same denomination.[5] They may arrive expecting their new church to be the same as–or better than–their previous church. Their conscious and unconscious expectations color their evaluation of their new church home.

Worshiper mobility and other issues contribute to diverse opinions in the congregation. Almost one in four worshipers is unaware of their congregation's vision or think the goals or directions are unclear. Views about the congregation's future divide worshipers: should we go back to the way we did things in the past, rethink where we are heading, or decide on new directions?[6]

Minority viewpoints collide with majority votes. Congregations now take democratic decision making to new heights, giving attendees multiple opportunities to participate. Almost all worshipers (94%) express satisfaction with their part in the congregation's decisions.[7] The 1960s saw the religious pluralism ideal expand beyond mere tolerance to a greater desire to respect individualism and minority opinions.[8] In previous decades, a majority vote required those expressing minority viewpoints to acquiesce quietly to majority rule. Although the desire to make decisions by majority vote in churches remains, decision makers are increasingly concerned about ensuring those with minority views are happy and feel valued. As a result, the door on any decision rarely closes firmly, and debates continue. Seeking consensus in all matters makes pastoral leadership more complicated and forward movement more perilous.

Many styles of leadership. Unfortunately, many people in the pews can recount painful chapters with previous pastors and lay staff leaders who took the church in directions that damaged relationships and ministries. Some members who complain about pastoral leadership may actually feel that the leadership they have is not what they believe the church needs.

The majority of worshipers describe their pastor or priest as one who inspires people to take action.[9] However, some worshipers prefer a proactive leadership style, in which the leader tends to take charge. In a few settings, a reactive style–leadership that acts on the goals that worshipers have set–prevails. Few churches operate in a pastoral leadership vacuum, in which the people in the pews initiate most activities.

In general, roughly half of worshipers feel strongly allied with the congregation's key leader. They report that there is a very good match between their church and their minister, pastor, or priest. Another third agree that the match is a good one. Unfortunately, however, a small number of dissatisfied people, especially if they hold lay leadership positions, can disrupt the harmony of church or parish life.[10]

Worshipers' satisfaction with their pastor varies from one congregation to another, in part because of the policies of the denomination or faith group. In faith groups that assign the congregation a pastor or priest–for example, Catholic parishes or Methodist churches–worshipers are less likely to view their leader as a good match.[11] Even within the same congregation, the pastor and the worshipers may hold different opinions. For example, Protestant *pastors* are less likely to see their leadership as a good match for the congregation than typical Protestant *worshipers.*[12]

Major redefinition of the pastoral role. Luther's early proclamations ran counter to the belief in ordained clergy as special mediators with God. As recently as 1982, a World Council of Churches document reaffirmed the widespread agreement that ministry is indeed the work of "the whole people of God."[13] Various writers document the long-standing negotiations between laity and clergy as they live out the priesthood of all believers.[14] The unique role that clergy play remains ambivalent.

Several major trends push the occupation of "pastor" in diverse directions. New categories of people entering ministry in large numbers–for example, women and second-career entrants–further amplify the ambiguity surrounding the clerical role. Female pastors and pastors with prior secular career experience bring alternative leadership models to the local church. Women now serve as the senior or solo pastor in one fourth of mainline Protestant churches. More than one third of full-time pastors currently serving in local churches worked in one or more occupations before entering ministry. Among recently ordained pastors (those entering the ministry in the past ten years), the average age at ordination is 43. This compares to an average ordination age of only 26 for pastors in ministry for three or more decades.[15]

The debate about ministry as a profession rather than a calling or office has raged for several decades.[16] Some writers argue that an increased emphasis on the professional model and credentialing led pastors away from their role as spiritual leaders. These writers believe that when pastors are evaluated on competency and acquired skills, ministry looks more like a profession in which pastors produce denominationally preferred outcomes. When leaders are encouraged to concentrate on how to make a difference in the world and be effective leaders, they have less time to be "made different" in their relationship with God.[17]

More small churches and fewer full-time pastors. Fewer worshipers today report attending worship services weekly. Over the course of an average month, the percentage of worshipers in attendance at all four weekend services is less than the percentage a decade ago.[18] The average church now has less than 100 people attending worship services. Congregations slipping below this critical number find funding even one full-time pastoral leader taxing. This results in changes in church staffing models from an emphasis on full-time ordained clergy to a greater reliance on part-time pastors and lay staff members.[19]

More demands on smaller budgets. One in three congregations now reports a declining financial base.[20] Yet church expenses continue to escalate. For many congregations, funding one or more staff positions includes providing salaries, housing allowances, health care benefits, and retirement plans. The costs of building maintenance, electricity, heating, and other basics further strain existing budgets–particularly for churches with aging facilities. In real dollars, many congregations raise more money than ever before, but their expenses far outpace the monies contributed.

Increasing pastoral stress and negative impact on health. As congregations shrink in membership size and resources, the pastoral role demands greater dexterity. Being asked to function at optimal levels, regardless of changing circumstances, tests even the most committed clergy. On occasion, ministers doubt their call to ministry. Doubts may arise, for example, when they receive criticism from members, there is lack of agreement about their role as pastor, they face excessive demands, or the ministry negatively affects family members.[21] Because of these doubts and demands, among other things, clergy are more likely than the average American to suffer from stress-related illnesses such as obesity, arthritis, diabetes, high blood pressure, and depression.[22]

National debates deflate local ministry. Arguments at the denominational level over marriage and ordination policies, clergy misconduct, and the leadership role of laity filter down to local churches. Conflicts at the national level distract from other ministry efforts and issues. Some individuals withhold pledges or withdraw from their church in protest, while some congregations drop or change their denominational affiliation. In extreme cases, the exodus of churches creates a large enough wave that new denominations arise. Regardless of how theologically central one views these discussions, the debates affect the vitality of local churches–through loss of members, contributions, and vision.

Disappearing generations in congregations. Worshipers are older on average than the U.S. population, but perhaps more important is the fact that the average worshiper today is older than the average worshiper in 2001 (54 vs. 51 years of age). The percentage of worshipers younger than 45 has dropped eight percentage points since 2001 (from 40% to only 32% in 2008).[23] Further, less than half of worshipers have children still living at home.[24] Thus fewer congregations include worshipers from all four generations living today. The absence of multiple generations in the pews profoundly alters present and future congregational vitality.[25]

Communication and media use diversifies. In a sea of professional specialists, the pastor's skill set reflects that of a "generalist," including the multiple roles of scholar, preacher, worship leader, teacher, spiritual leader, counselor, church administrator, and community leader. Now every savvy pastor must adapt to new social media and worship technology that calls for yet other skills. The explosion of innovative communication technologies strains the budgets and imaginations of many congregations and their leaders. It also raises new boundary and ethical issues for leaders to navigate with members and community residents.

A New Landscape for Pastoral Ministry

Whether the Franklin Downtown Church or Pastor Chris realize it or not, new realities profoundly shape their choices and future decisions. A new call will test Chris's leadership skills in more ways than he can anticipate. Lay leaders likely hold unrealistic expectations about the congregation's membership growth and its long-term financial sustainability. Now more than ever, pastors and church leaders need strong partnerships based on clear expectations and mutual respect.

Our concern with pastors and congregations points to the significance of ministry itself. We agree with Daniel Aleshire's assertion that "ministry is never about the minister; it is always about the gospel the minister proclaims."[26] We hope that our lens brings into sharper focus what it takes for pastors, lay leaders, and churches to declare the gospel today.

Questions for Pastors

- Looking back over your years in pastoral ministry, which one or two trends (out of the ten broad issues outlined in this chapter) have had the most impact on your ministry?
- As you reflect on your current situation, what do you see as the trends most affecting the congregation's ministry effectiveness?

Questions for Lay Leaders

- Looking back over the past ten years, what trends have had the most impact on the congregation's ministry effectiveness?
- As you reflect on the congregation's future, what trends do you see as presenting the greatest challenges and opportunities?

Chapter 2

What Kind of Pastor?

Pastors live with tensions of many stripes; they seek to lead spiritual lives yet work to address the grittiest human problems, live normal lives with families and financial security yet serve as models of self-sacrifice, and find happiness and satisfaction yet resist the trappings of professional success. These and other tensions explain in part why "priests and ministers in almost every period of American history view their office as a calling in crisis."[1] Who is called to parish ministry now compared to the past surfaces another tension. As the age, gender, training, and experience of pastors shift, what congregations can expect when they call a new minister is a moving target. In this chapter, we outline the profile of pastors in basic terms: their demographics, theological training, and employment characteristics such as compensation and benefits. This is the first step in answering the question, what kind of pastor for what kind of congregation? As a group of lay leaders grapple with a pastoral transition, their decisions confirm the importance of this question.

Pines Community Church

The congregation prided itself on being a community anchor. Previous pastors were involved in the town's many activities. Because that is all the members had ever known, they assumed all pastors were church leaders *and* community leaders. The pastoral search committee was eager to get started on their task of finding a new pastor. Any step that might delay them seemed a waste of precious time. They feared the months between pastors could deplete resources and members' energy. Ed, the congregation's patriarch, insisted that the lay leaders produce a document that described the church's current circumstances—their membership, church school, adult education, and finances. Some leaders resisted Ed's advice. Susan believed that if they were too honest about what was really going in the church, they would not be able to convince a good pastor to come. Her argument that "showing our warts" was detrimental to the church's quest for a new pastor was persuasive to many. After a great deal of discussion, the committee compromised on a written summary of the church's mission and needs—a description that highlighted the congregation's most positive features.

Ted was not looking for a new call. He and his family enjoyed their church, their friends in the community, and the kids' activities and schools. One day Ted received an e-mail from Allen, an old family friend. The e-mail began with memories of Ted's father but ended with a surprising question: Would Ted consider serving in another congregation? Allen believed Ted had all the pastoral gifts and qualities that were needed at the church where Allen currently attended—Pines Community Church. Receiving this unexpected request from someone who knew him so well was hard to ignore. After discussion with his wife, he answered Allen's e-mail with a request for more information. Perhaps this congregation really needed him.

Demographic Profile of Pastors

Pastoral ministry envelops a wide range of personalities, skill sets, theological viewpoints, and definitions of ministry. Each congregation draws on a pastor candidate pool that is more diverse than in the past. Lay leaders need to be aware of the unique profile and pathway to ministry for pastoral leaders in their denomination or faith group. Here we map out demographic differences between three major religious denominational groups: mainline Protestant pastors, conservative Protestant pastors, and Catholic priests.[2]

Gender. Male pastors still outnumber female pastors in Christian faith traditions. Only men can serve as ordained Catholic priests, but women play an important role as lay leaders in small parishes and lay associate pastors in larger parishes. Male pastors lead in most conservative Protestant churches as well.[3] The entry of women into ministry in many mainline Protestant traditions has grown more pronounced in the past two decades. Now women serve as the senior or solo pastor in three out of ten of such churches (see Figure 2.1).

Figure 2.1
Male Ordained Clergy by Denominational Tradition

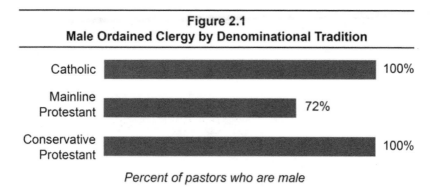

Percent of pastors who are male

Previous research suggests—and denominational staff and pastors themselves often comment on—the unique experiences of women pastors. In later chapters, we explore whether women serving in local churches experience greater stress, more role conflict, or less satisfaction with ministry.

Marital status. Because Catholic priests are not allowed to marry, our description of marriage and family patterns applies to Protestant pastors only. The majority of Protestant pastors are in their first marriage (see Figure 2.2). However, some pastors have remarried after divorce or the death of a spouse. Mainline Protestant pastors are twice as likely as conservative Protestant pastors to be remarried after divorce (20% compared to 10%). While the percentages are small, mainline Protestant clergy are also more than four times as likely to be divorced or separated (9% compared to 2%).

The marital status of female mainline Protestant pastors is more diverse than that of men serving such churches (see Figure 2.3). More female than male pastors are divorced or separated (one in four female pastors) or never

Figure 2.2
Marital Status of Protestant Pastors

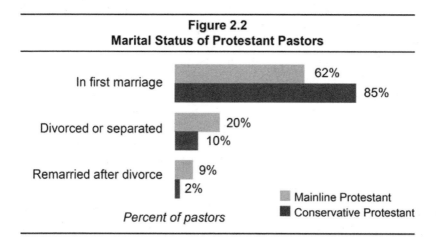

Percent of pastors

Figure 2.3
Marital Status of Mainline Protestant Pastors by Gender

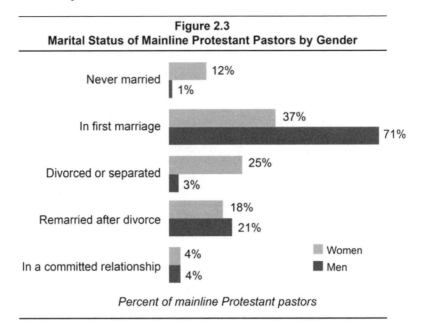

Percent of mainline Protestant pastors

married (about one in ten female pastors). However, women and men are about equally likely to be remarried after divorce or to be in a committed relationship. Some congregations resist calling a female pastor or a pastor who is unmarried, as many female pastors are. This diminishes the range of settings where some women pastors can find employment.

Married pastors may have spouses who work and contribute to household income. The majority of married pastors have a spouse (or committed partner) who works full- or part-time: 70% of mainline Protestant pastors have working spouses/partners compared to 60% of conservative Protestant pastors.

Family composition. Mainline Protestant pastors have a median number of two children, while conservative Protestant pastors have three children on average (median). The majority of these children are older and no longer live at home (64% of mainline Protestant pastors have no children living at home, compared to 51% of conservative Protestant pastors). The typical family profile of pastors is linked to the age and life stage of pastors currently serving local congregations. We turn to those age profiles next.

Age. The median age of pastors is 55. Pastors are on average older today than pastors were in 2001, when the median age was only 51.[4] Thus the average age of pastors serving in local congregations climbed four years in less than a decade.

For several decades now, clergy serving in congregations have been growing older. In 1968, for example, 56% of mainline clergy and 54% of conservative Protestant clergy were younger than 45.[5] The shifting age profile of American clergy stems from several trends. Fewer young people have been entering seminary or ministry immediately following their undergraduate college graduation. Between 1962 and 2005, the average age of entering theological students rose by more than ten years.[6] Other research reveals that older seminary students often show more interest than younger students in serving as local church pastors.[7] Finally, more local church pastors today are "second career"–entering parish ministry after a career in another field or even retirement. Female pastors sometimes enter ministry after family responsibilities lessen or after an earlier sense of call was thwarted by church policies that prevented women's ordination.

The average age of pastors differs by denominational tradition, with Catholic priests being the oldest group (median age of 59). Catholic priests also had the oldest age profile in 2001 (median age of 56). Catholic priests today are concentrated in the 50-and-older age groups–especially the 60-and-older age group (half of all the priests in the sample). More mainline Protestant pastors fall in the 50-to-59 age group. More conservative Protestant pastors than others are found in the 40-to-49 age group. Overall, fewer than one in ten pastors today are under age 40 (see Figure 2.4).

Educational and Theological Profile of Pastors

Pastors bring diverse religious, educational, and career histories to their ministry. Some grew up involved in church life, but others did not. Some knew they were called to ministry at a young age, but others answered the call after working in another field. We explore these histories now.

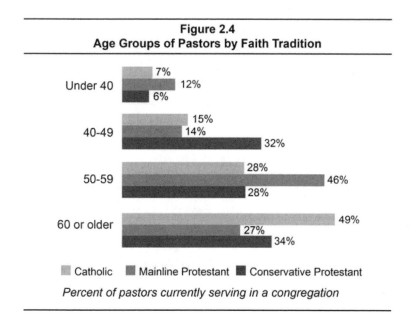

Figure 2.4
Age Groups of Pastors by Faith Tradition

Under 40
7%
12%
6%

40-49
15%
14%
32%

50-59
28%
46%
28%

60 or older
49%
27%
34%

■ Catholic ■ Mainline Protestant ■ Conservative Protestant

Percent of pastors currently serving in a congregation

Religious background. More than half of conservative Protestant pastors (59%) were raised in a different denomination than their current one. Further, few conservative Protestant pastors (one in three) actually switched their affiliation from another faith group (a mainline Protestant or Catholic tradition) to a conservative Protestant denomination. Mainline Protestant pastors are more likely to be currently serving in the denomination in which they were raised (56% remain in the same denomination). Only one in four mainline Protestant pastors has changed faith groups since his or her youth. Almost all Catholic priests (96%) were raised as Catholics.

Theological education. Most pastors come to parish ministry equipped with theological education. The Association of Theological Schools in the United States and Canada lists more than 260 institutions that offer post-baccalaureate programs to prepare pastors for ministry. Because a school's theological orientation is central to its program, each school or seminary thinks about the preparation for ministry in different ways.[8] Thus the amount and theological orientation of a pastor's education shapes his or her ministry.

The Catholic Church and mainline Protestant denominations have most often defined the appropriate training for pastors as an advanced theology degree after baccalaureate study. In contrast, many conservative Protestant groups created their own Bible colleges and other centers for preparing pastors to serve in local churches. As Figure 2.5 indicates, almost all Catholic priests and mainline Protestant pastors hold an advanced theology degree of some kind–typically, the Master of Divinity. However, a small minority have obtained a Doctor of Ministry degree or other theological doctoral

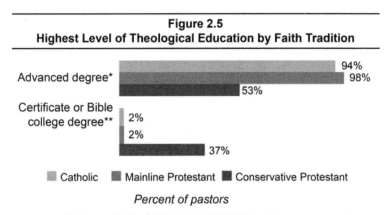

Figure 2.5
Highest Level of Theological Education by Faith Tradition

Advanced degree*
94%
98%
53%

Certificate or Bible college degree**
2%
2%
37%

■ Catholic   ■ Mainline Protestant   ■ Conservative Protestant

Percent of pastors

*Master of Divinity (M.Div.), Bachelor of Divinity, other master's degree, or doctorate including Doctor of Ministry degree, Ph.D. or Th.D.

**Certificate from denominational training program, Bible college, or seminary

NOTE: Remainder of pastors have no theological education.

degree. On the other hand, only half of conservative Protestant pastors hold an advanced theology degree. Almost four in ten conservative Protestant pastors have obtained a Bible college degree.[9]

Ordination for ministry. Most faith traditions confer a special status or office to persons believed to possess the gifts for ministry. Ordination indicates that the pastor's activities are being carried out "officially" and are sanctioned by the local faith community and the larger religious body.[10] The rites of ordination carry significant meaning for the pastor and faith community. In general, people do not serve as full-time pastors until they have met all the requirements for receiving ordination. Almost all pastors participating in this project were ordained at the time of the study (98% of Catholic priests, 92% of mainline Protestant pastors, and 97% of conservative Protestant pastors).[11]

Historically, people entered seminary immediately after their undergraduate education was completed. But as we noted earlier, as the overall age at ordination shifts, so does the age profile of pastors. The older pastors are when they are ordained, the fewer years they can serve as local church pastors before retirement. On average, pastors have already served 23 years in ministry. Catholic priests report 31 years of ministry, on average, compared to only 22 years for mainline Protestant and 24 years for conservative Protestant pastors. However, given the increasing number of second-career clergy, the typical length of time Protestant pastors serve over their lifetime is certain to decrease.

Second-career pastors. Less than half of pastors (44%) worked full-time at one or more occupations before entering the ministry. Protestant pastors are more than twice as likely as Catholic priests to be second-career pastors (45% of mainline pastors and 47% of conservative pastors, compared to only 22% of Catholic priests).[12]

We track the second-career trend in another way by looking at one possible outcome: the average age at ordination among pastors. We note an upward trend in the ordination age of those entering ministry. Those who entered the ministry more recently (serving less than ten years) were substantially older when they were ordained than long-term clergy (those serving for more than ten years). For example, the average age of first-decade clergy at the time of their ordination is over 35 in all faith groups (average age of 40 for Catholic priests, 44 for mainline Protestant pastors, and 37 for conservative Protestant pastors). In contrast, pastors in their fourth decade of ministry—regardless of faith group—were ordained (on average) at age 26 (see Figure 2.6).

Number of parish ministry positions. Because Catholic priests are older and have been in ministry longer than Protestant pastors on average, they also tend to serve in more parish settings over the course of their ministry careers. In addition, bishops make the decisions about where Catholic priests will serve and for how long. Thus Catholic priests move from parish to parish more frequently than Protestant pastors, at present having served

Figure 2.6: Average age of pastors at ordination by years in ministry and denominational tradition

Decade in Ministry	First	Second	Third	Fourth
Years in Ministry	< 10	10–20	21–30	31+
Catholic	40	30	29	26
Mainline Protestant	44	37	28	26
Conservative Protestant	37	36	29	26

a median of five parishes compared to four for mainline Protestant pastors and only three for conservative Protestant pastors.[13]

First-call pastors. One quarter of conservative Protestant pastors are currently serving in their first call, while only 5% of Catholic priests and 13% of mainline Protestant pastors are. As more pastors begin ministry later in their life, pastors will gain experience from fewer parish settings over their career.

Typical, but Not Typical

In some ways, Robert seems like a typical conservative Protestant pastor. He is married with four children and has another on the way. But he recently received his Ph.D.—unusual among conservative Protestant pastors. In addition to preaching every week, leading Bible study, and attending to other pastoral responsibilities, Robert coaches his daughters' soccer team, works in the yard, and fires up the grill for friends and neighbors. He balances the intensity of pastoral work with time for recreation and family.

Profile of Current Pastoral Call

The previous pastoral profiles apply to the past: career history, educational history, and personal history. Now we turn to the ministry settings where pastors serve currently.

More than one church or more than one job. The majority of pastors serve one congregation. But one in four Catholic priests pastors multiple parishes. A multipoint or yoked parish assignment is not the usual arrangement for Protestant pastors (12% of mainline Protestant pastors and 6% of conservative Protestant pastors serve more than one church). A more common pattern among conservative Protestant pastors is to be a tentmaker or bivocational pastor–holding down a secular job *and* a ministry position. More than one in four conservative Protestant pastors (30%) work as tentmakers, but only 1% of Catholic priests and 6% of mainline Protestant pastors do.

Senior or solo pastor. Three out of four congregations have just one full-time ordained pastor. However, nonordained ministerial staff also supply leadership for a few congregations. Half of the pastors describe their current position as the solo pastor. Conservative Protestant pastors are far more likely to report they are the senior pastor or minister (70% do so compared to only 31% of mainline pastors and 51% of Catholic priests).[14]

Full- or part-time employment. Almost all Catholic priests (96%) serve as full-time pastors in one or more parishes. The majority of Protestant pastors serve full-time as well (85% of mainline Protestant pastors and 83% of conservative Protestant pastors). Full-time employment often translates into a higher salary, a manse or housing allowance, health care benefits, and contributions to a retirement plan.

Total compensation. In addition to an annual salary, compensation for pastors often includes housing assistance, in the form of a manse or parsonage and/or a housing allowance.

Figure 2.7 displays the total compensation for pastors. The salary structure for Catholic priests is a flat one; compensation does not vary much by the size of the parish (median of $35,220 annually). However, clergy compensation is more closely tied to congregational size among Protestant groups. On average, mainline Protestant pastors earn more than their conservative Protestant colleagues ($54,530 median annual compensation vs. $49,758 for conservative Protestant pastors) despite serving churches with similar median numbers in worship (mainline Protestant churches averaging 82 worshipers; conservative Protestant churches averaging 90 worshipers).

Housing provisions. Almost all Catholic priests (94%) are furnished housing by the parish. But the practice of providing pastoral housing occurs

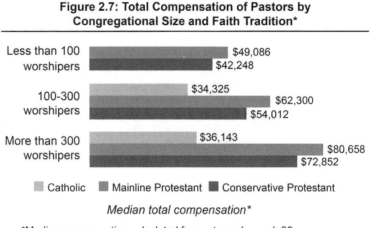

Figure 2.7: Total Compensation of Pastors by Congregational Size and Faith Tradition*

Less than 100 worshipers: $49,086 / $42,248

100-300 worshipers: $34,325 / $62,300 / $54,012

More than 300 worshipers: $36,143 / $80,658 / $72,852

■ Catholic ■ Mainline Protestant ■ Conservative Protestant

*Median total compensation**

*Median compensation calculated for pastors who work 30 or more hours per week for the congregation.

in only a minority of mainline Protestant churches (40%) and conservative Protestant churches (26%). Instead, two out of three pastors serving in mainline Protestant churches and six in ten in conservative Protestant churches receive a housing allowance (see Figure 2.8).

Health insurance. A majority of pastors receive health insurance as a benefit of their congregational employment, either from the congregation or from the denomination. However, in conservative Protestant churches, only slightly more than half of pastors receive health insurance benefits from the congregation or denomination (see Figure 2.9).

More than half of married mainline Protestant pastors report that their spouse and children also receive health care coverage through the

Figure 2.8
Housing Provisions: Pastors with a Manse or Housing Allowance

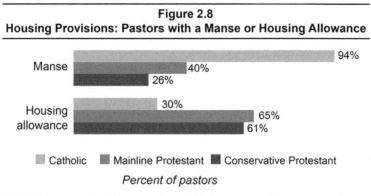

Percent of pastors

NOTE: Percentages add to more than 100% because some pastors receive both housing and a housing allowance.

Figure 2.9: Health Care Insurance Provided by Congregation or Denomination for Pastor, Spouse, and Children

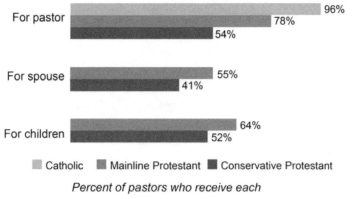

Percent of pastors who receive each

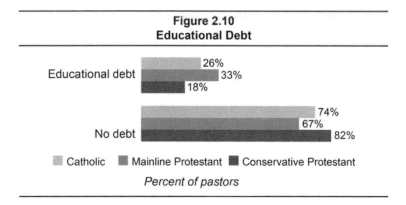

Figure 2.10
Educational Debt

Educational debt — 26% Catholic, 33% Mainline Protestant, 18% Conservative Protestant

No debt — 74% Catholic, 67% Mainline Protestant, 82% Conservative Protestant

Catholic ▪ Mainline Protestant ▪ Conservative Protestant

Percent of pastors

congregation or denomination. Among mainline and conservative Protestant pastors, more receive health care coverage for their children than for their spouse.

Contributions to a retirement plan. Their congregation or denomination contributes to a retirement plan for the majority of Catholic priests (78%) and mainline Protestant pastors (84%). However, less than half of conservative Protestant pastors (47%) receive this benefit.

With regard to benefits—housing support, health care coverage, and retirement plan contributions—conservative Protestant pastors receive less support from their church or denomination than pastors in other faith groups.

Educational debt. Only one out of four Catholic leaders carries educational debt. In contrast, about one third of mainline pastors bear educational debt, and these pastors make the highest median monthly payments toward that debt. Compared to other pastors, conservative Protestant pastors are less likely to hold an advanced theology degree. Thus it is not surprising that only 18% of these pastors carry any level of educational debt (see Figure 2.10).

Statistically, the typical Catholic priest

- is male,
- is 59 years old,
- holds an advanced theology degree,
- is ordained,
- has served 31 years in ministry,
- has served in five parishes, and
- lives in parish housing.

But Father James—at 42 years of age—is fresh out of seminary. He felt the call to ministry after working several years as a social worker. He's beginning his pastoral ministry as an associate priest with a desire to serve the church for a lifetime.

Statistically, the typical mainline Protestant pastor

- is male (seven in ten are male),
- is 55 years old,
- holds an advanced theology degree,
- is ordained,
- has served 22 years in ministry,
- has served in four churches, and
- is provided a housing allowance.

In contrast, Pastor Ellen has just started a new call as solo pastor of her second church after seven years in ministry. She lives with her daughter in a small manse not far from the church and struggles financially with a limited compensation package and ongoing student debt.

Statistically, the typical conservative Protestant pastor

- is male,
- is 54 years old,
- might hold an advanced theological degree (half do),
- is ordained,
- has served 24 years in ministry,
- has served in three churches, and
- is provided a housing allowance.

Pastor Jared doesn't fit this profile, however. He is ordained, but he's now serving his sixth congregation after almost 30 years in ministry. He remarried recently; his first wife died several years ago. Unlike many conservative Protestant pastors, he was raised in the denomination he now serves.

What Kind of Pastor for Our Congregation?

A group of lay leaders at Pines Community Church began reviewing candidates. Their pool was quite diverse—some pastors nearing retirement, others seeking their first call. Some were second-career pastors and others had experience as associate pastors. A few made theological statements far outside the lay leaders' comfort zone. After a lengthy discussion, the review committee came up with criteria to shorten the list. They promised to pray about it and bring the names of their top three choices for pastors when they met again. At their next meeting, the group tallied the votes. To their surprise, two pastors received a large number of the votes. Both pastors looked promising: one pastor's recommendations said he was a strong preacher with an outgoing personality; the other pastor's said she was second-generation clergy, strong in preaching and teaching, and recognized widely in the denomination for her leadership skills. The committee was thrilled to have two good choices. Then Ted's family friend, Allen, suggested a third candidate. He argued that because the group had not identified a third candidate, he would like to recommend Ted as a possibility. After Allen told them about Ted's background, the group agreed that making Ted the third option was a good idea. Allen notified Ted that the church wanted him to come for an interview. He confided in Ted that two other strong candidates had been invited to talk with church leaders as well. When Ted reviewed the church's materials, he didn't find them helpful. He thought they left so much out, he couldn't even read between the lines. He wondered, "Surely the church can't be that perfect!"

The routes to pastoral ministry are as diverse as the people who take the journey. Pastors vary in age, gender, theological training, preparation for ministry, and experience. Some find full-time employment in one congregation; others hold responsibility for several parishes. Still others juggle their ministry role with secular jobs. Pastors also differ in the benefits and support for them and their families that their congregation provides. One certainty is clear: a "typical" or average pastor does not exist.

As congregational leaders consider what kind of pastor would be the best match for their congregation, church size and faith tradition influence staffing arrangements. However, congregational leaders should also consider what type of pastor will best help them realize their future ministry goals. What pastoral profile is right for where the congregation is heading?

Stable and numerically declining congregations find that adopting alternative staffing plans enables them to expand their outreach and ministries. The shifting age and career patterns of pastors give congregations additional options for making better matches than in the past. In future chapters, we investigate whether the topics considered in this chapter—the pastor's personal characteristics and educational or career history—influence a pastor's ministry satisfaction and overall well-being.

Questions for Pastors

- How do your religious background, theological education, work experiences prior to entering ministry, or various ministry experiences relate to your leadership strengths? How would you describe these linkages in conversations about a potential new church call?

- If you were candid with leaders in the new congregation, what personal factors (such as family or compensation needs and health or retirement issues) does the church need to hear about early in the process?

Questions for Lay Leaders

- Looking back over the years, what previous pastors were exceptionally capable and what did they do best? Do you know the source of their strengths?
- Be candid: Are there some pastors you would prefer not to consider because of their age, gender, marital or family profile, educational background, theology, or something else? Based on your experiences, why do such characteristics detract from potential candidates? What personality traits or previous experiences would a pastor need to have?

THE REVEREND BOB™ LEADERSHIP FRANCHISE,
BACKED BY AGGRESSIVE ADVERTISING AND A
"CHURCH GROWTH GUARANTEE"®, GREW RAPIDLY.
WITHIN FIVE YEARS, NEARLY ONE IN FOUR
CHURCH LEADERS, NATIONALLY, WAS A "BOB"™

Chapter 3

What Kind of Congregation?

Half of American adults, or 105 million people, report attending a religious service in the past year.[1] However, fewer than one in four Americans attend services in any given week.[2] When Americans attend any of the more than 300,000 congregations across the country, they encounter particular congregational characteristics and attributes. For understanding what makes the best fit between a pastoral leader and the church context, identifying common church profiles is necessary. In this chapter, we describe the key differences between congregations that will help us better recognize the best leader-congregation matches. But first, we recount the pastoral transition of a Catholic parish and its new priest. The congregation's Catholic affiliation, large size, and location frame the kind of leadership-fit issues likely to arise.

St. Mary's Catholic Parish

Nestled in the hills of a sprawling suburb, the parish church of St. Mary's remained the most visible of the area's six Catholic churches. The church's French Gothic tower stood watch over the changing community. Once considered a missionary outpost, the recent influx of more affluent residents created renewed hope for longtime members. The parish's reputation for courage came from their many strategies for adventurous outreach. During one late Spring Mass, Father Thomas announced that he was being appointed to another parish and that the archbishop had selected a new pastor for the parish. Although the parishioners felt some sadness about Father

Thomas's departure, they trusted the bishop to appoint a pastor who might have fresh ideas about reaching out to the community's newcomers.

On the following Monday, St. Mary's lay staff huddled in the business manager's office. Elizabeth, a former sister and the director of religious education, spoke first: "Do you think the new pastor will be as easy-going as Father Thomas?" Teresa, the parish administrator, tried not to shout: "Are you kidding, no one could be that laid-back!" After a round of "What's the worst that could happen?" predictions, the business manager sighed. "We'll just have to pray and hope we get a good priest—one who sees *us* as part of a ministry team."

Father John knew in high school that serving the Church would be his lifetime passion. After graduation, he attended a Catholic university and then seminary. As one of the best and brightest seminarians, Father John was able to continue his studies in Rome after ordination, earning a doctorate. Upon his return to the United States, the archbishop appointed him to an urban parish as an associate pastor. He reveled in all the ministry opportunities, working in a thriving lay ministry formation program, a neighborhood clinic, and strong youth and singles ministries. In his third year after ordination, the archbishop appointed Father John as pastoral administrator in a northern urban neighborhood. This community faced more daunting economic distress and racial tensions than Father John's first appointment. Yet he found working among struggling families, always on the border between hope and ruin, profoundly meaningful. He served tirelessly because he could "see the face of God in the faces of his neighbors." Two years later, a third letter arrived from the archbishop, appointing him as St. Mary's new pastor. For the first time, Father John would be *the* pastor of a parish! All his education, training, and parish experiences had prepared him for this day.

What Is the Denomination or Faith Group Affiliation?

Most congregations (98%) cite an affiliation with a denomination, convention, or other association. The number of U.S. denominations and religious bodies exceeds 200, with the exact figure fluctuating as groups merge, divide, and dissolve. In our analyses, we use the faith group categories generally followed in the social sciences. (Appendix 3 lists all denominations with which participating pastors are affiliated.) The three broad faith groups included here are Catholic parishes, conservative Protestant churches, and mainline Protestant churches.[3]

The largest single group of U.S. churches, which reports more than 68 million members in more than 19,000 parishes, continues to be those affiliated with the Catholic Church.[4] The most recent statistical report indicates that annual Catholic membership grew 1.5%, outpacing U.S. population growth. The sheer number of these parishes–and their associated priests, pastoral leaders, and worshipers–significantly shapes American culture and politics.[5]

The second-largest group of U.S. churches is conservative Protestant congregations. Five of the ten largest denominations fit in the conservative Protestant category: Southern Baptist Convention (16 million adherents in more than 40,000 churches), Church of God in Christ (5.5 million adherents in more than 15,000 churches), National Baptist Convention (USA) (5 million adherents in 9,000 churches), National Baptist Convention of America (3.5 million adherents in 2,500 churches), and Assemblies of God (2.9 million adherents in 12,000 churches).[6] Many of these denominations, and individual congregations within those denominations, continue to grow numerically.

Despite decades of membership decline, mainline Protestant denominations remain a major presence in the American religious landscape. Three mainline denominations–United Methodist Church, Evangelical Lutheran Church in America, and Presbyterian Church (USA)–rank in the top ten largest denominations. Mainline denominations account for one fourth of the 25 largest denominations. In addition to the three named above, other large groups include the American Baptist Churches, the Episcopal Church, and the United Church of Christ.[7]

In subsequent chapters, faith group differences illustrate how theology and tradition set the stage for pastoral ministry.

What about Church Size?

The elephant in the room is often the number of participants in the worshiping community. Many congregations imagine that their size makes them unique and exempt from patterns found in other churches. One of the most-often-used hedges against making positive changes is size: "We're too small," "We're too big," or "Our church used to be larger and back then we could do more things well." Many observers assume that large churches have all the advantages–more staff, more money, more volunteers, and better facilities. Do small, midsize, and larger congregations need different types of leaders and alternative models of leadership to be effective? Yes, they often do.

We can look at congregational size in many ways: average worship attendance, number of participants in small groups or other congregational programs and ministries, and financial resources. Figure 3.1 illustrates some dimensions of church size. The largest numbers reflect the total number of people associated with the congregation in any way: this includes adults and children, members and nonmembers, and everyone from regular participants to one-time visitors. This yardstick yields 277 as

Figure 3.1: Sizes of U.S. congregations

Number of people (median):	All Congregations	Catholic	Mainline Protestant	Conservative Protestant
Associated in any way with the congregation	277	2,322	168	249
Regularly participating in the congregation	130	831	117	120
Adults (over age 18) regularly participating	85	678	70	80
Average worship attendance	95	650	82	90

the median size of U.S. congregations and parishes. Although this figure gives us some idea about the breadth or scope of ministry, it only hints at the level of regular participation. Because Catholic parishes claim any registered Catholic family or individual within the parish's geographic boundaries, the median number of people associated with a parish (2,322) is substantially larger than the numbers associated with Protestant churches (a median of 249 in conservative churches compared to a median of 168 for mainline churches).

Using the number of people who regularly participate in congregational life reduces the median size to 130 across all congregations, 831 for Catholic parishes, and around 120 for both mainline and conservative Protestant churches. A considerable gap exists between the number of people touched by the congregation in any way and the number of people who regularly attend services. Typically, worship attendance is about 50% of the membership.[8]

While there are many ways to measure church size or scope of ministry, our previous work informs our decision to choose a single strategy for our analyses: the average worship attendance (which often includes teenagers and children).[9] In some cases, designating size categories is also helpful for making comparisons. We define *small* churches as worshiping communities with fewer than 100 in average attendance. *Midsize* congregations and parishes average between 100 and 300 in worship attendance. *Large* churches draw more than 300 people to worship (see Figure 3.2).

The majority of Protestant congregations are small. In contrast, most Catholic parishes (76%) average more than 300 in their weekend services. Relatively few Protestant churches (only 7 to 8%) welcome that many

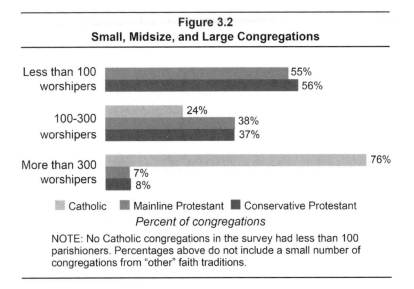

Figure 3.2
Small, Midsize, and Large Congregations

Less than 100 worshipers
55%
56%

100-300 worshipers
24%
38%
37%

More than 300 worshipers
76%
7%
8%

▨ Catholic ▧ Mainline Protestant ■ Conservative Protestant
Percent of congregations

NOTE: No Catholic congregations in the survey had less than 100 parishioners. Percentages above do not include a small number of congregations from "other" faith traditions.

worshipers. Despite media attention to megachurches, the religious land-scape in America is dotted with many, many small houses of worship. A wide gap exists between where the largest numbers of people worship and the size of the typical congregation. This gap means that most regular worshipers attend larger churches, but most churches are small.[10]

In subsequent chapters, we examine the impact of congregational size on pastors' experiences in ministry–their levels of satisfaction, physical and emotional health, and job stress.

Is Worship Attendance Growing, Stable, or Declining?

A congregation changes size over time. Nothing dictates a particular cycle of attendance growth, stability, or decline. Many new churches grow, but not all. In fact, the failure rate of new congregations exceeds 30% in many denominations.[11] And some congregations that are hundreds of years old attract new worshipers and grow numerically.

Unfortunately, most U.S. congregations are not growing in worship attendance.[12] Over a five-year period from 2003 to 2008, *half* of the congregations participating in the U.S. Congregational Life Survey declined in worship attendance by more than 5%. Less than one in five reported that their worship attendance grew by more than 5%. The remaining congregations (27%) occupied the stable category–neither growing nor declining by more than 5% over the same five-year period (see Figure 3.3).

Protestant churches were more likely to decline numerically than Catholic parishes. One in three Catholic parishes had stable attendance in services (see Figure 3.3).

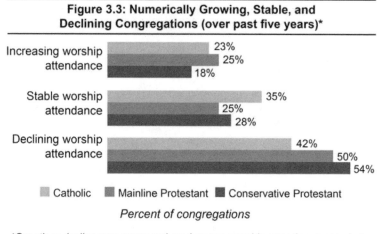

Figure 3.3: Numerically Growing, Stable, and Declining Congregations (over past five years)*

Increasing worship attendance: Catholic 23%, Mainline Protestant 25%, Conservative Protestant 18%

Stable worship attendance: Catholic 35%, Mainline Protestant 25%, Conservative Protestant 28%

Declining worship attendance: Catholic 42%, Mainline Protestant 50%, Conservative Protestant 54%

Catholic   Mainline Protestant   Conservative Protestant

Percent of congregations

*Growth or decline was measured as: Average worship attendance reported in 2008 minus average worship attendance reported in 2003, the difference divided by 2003 average attendance. Congregations growing more than 5% between 2003 and 2008 were designated as "growing"; congregations experiencing a decline of more than 5% were categorized as "declining"; remaining congregations were placed in the "stable"category.

In subsequent chapters, we look at leaders in growing, stable, and declining congregations to evaluate the part pastors play in promoting growth.

Full-Time Pastor or None at All?

All but 2% of congregations employ some paid staff, either part-time or full-time. Just one full-time, ordained pastor leads three out of four congregations. Nonordained ministerial staff supply additional leadership in many congregations, with larger congregations more often benefiting from multiple staff.[13] Figure 3.4 shows the average number of full-time employees who are ordained professionals and other pastoral leaders by size of church. Additional full-time employees in other categories (e.g., clerical or custodial) serve in one in three churches.

Figure 3.4: Median number of ordained clergy and pastoral leaders by congregational size

	Number of pastoral leaders *
Fewer than 100 in worship	1.0
100–300 in worship	1.5
More than 300 in worship	3.5

*Full-time equivalent ordained professionals and pastoral leaders.

As congregations pursue alternative staffing models, faith group tradition comes into play. Some congregations share a pastor with one or more other congregations (sometimes called yoked or multipoint parishes). One in four priests takes responsibility for more than one parish church. Multipoint situations are also more common among mainline than conservative Protestant churches (see Figure 3.5).

The ability of a pastor to serve well is constrained by yet another factor—some pastors hold down another job. While relatively rare, bivocational or "tentmaker" pastors crop up more frequently in conservative Protestant congregations than elsewhere (see Figure 3.5).

Church size is an important factor in church staffing. More small congregations resort to sharing a pastor with another congregation (multipoint parishes) or tentmaker strategies because they have fewer resources to pay a full-time pastor.

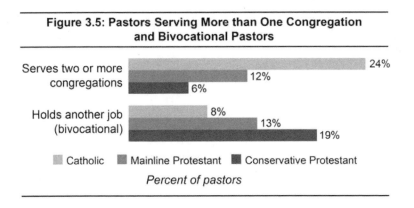

Figure 3.5: Pastors Serving More than One Congregation and Bivocational Pastors

Serves two or more congregations: 24%, 12%, 6%

Holds another job (bivocational): 8%, 13%, 19%

Catholic | Mainline Protestant | Conservative Protestant

Percent of pastors

Where Is the Congregation Located?

Congregational strengths and challenges sometimes result from the geographic area served. Just as there are assets within the congregation (people, their talents, and their monetary contributions), the community offers resources as well. Different types of communities offer distinct ministry prospects to congregations. Churches succeed when they draw on and address the unique opportunities available in their community.[14] We asked pastors to describe the type of community where the church or parish is located: a rural area, town or small city (fewer than 250,000 people), suburb of a large metropolitan area, or large metropolitan area (more than 250,000 people).

Rural area. Characterized by low population density and high stability, these communities tend to have fewer young people, more people employed in farming and construction, and fewer college graduates. The community's stability generates some positives for faith communities and their leaders, but there are relatively few new residents to welcome into the church.

Town or small city (fewer than 250,000 people). Residents enjoy more employment and social opportunities in these communities. This category includes a broader range of economic conditions. Some small towns or cities depend on only one major employer. As long as that company or industry does well, the town prospers too. Without greater employment diversity, churches in these communities can experience economic distress when large employers leave town. The average age of residents in small cities tends to be older, as young people move away to seek opportunities in larger places.

Suburbs of a large metropolitan area. Typically, suburbs are growing in comparison to most rural areas and small towns. Primarily traditional families–married couples, some with children living at home–reside in the suburbs. Well-educated adults often work in professional and managerial positions. The majority of residents own their home rather than rent. Unemployment and poverty rates generally stay below the national average.

Large metropolitan area (more than 250,000 people). Large cities contain neighborhoods with great disparities in social and economic conditions. Well-educated, highly mobile young professionals, who rent rather than own homes, populate pockets of the city. Other neighborhoods mirror the economic hardships experienced by individuals and families who live there. In large metropolitan areas, population density is high and so is poverty and unemployment. More immigrants and racial-ethnic minorities reside in large population centers.

As Figure 3.6 illustrates, about half of Protestant churches are located in towns or small cities. One out of three conservative Protestant pastors

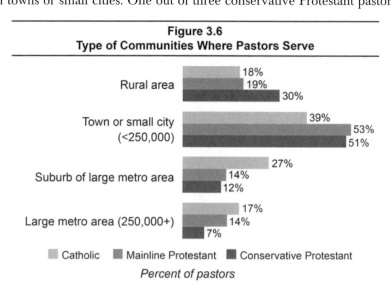

Figure 3.6
Type of Communities Where Pastors Serve

Rural area
18%
19%
30%

Town or small city (<250,000)
39%
53%
51%

Suburb of large metro area
27%
14%
12%

Large metro area (250,000+)
17%
14%
7%

■ Catholic   ■ Mainline Protestant   ■ Conservative Protestant
Percent of pastors

serves in a rural area. More Catholic priests than Protestant pastors serve in large metropolitan areas or their suburbs (44%).

Profile of Congregations

- Most churches are small with fewer than 100 worshipers.
- Catholic parishes are typically much larger than Protestant churches.
- In most congregations, worship attendance has remained the same or declined in recent years.
- Most congregations have one full-time paid pastor.
- A majority are located in rural areas or small towns and cities.
- Most report some conflict.
- Most churches exhibit three to five ministry strengths.

Congregations vary widely from this overview of what is typical. Franklin Downtown Church, for example, averages 225 in worship. Though still a small church, worship attendance at Pines Community Church has been increasing in recent years. St. Mary's, on the other hand, is located in the suburbs of a large city.

Is There Conflict?

Unfortunately, church discussions and decisions sometimes lead to conflict. Important issues and emerging challenges require thoughtful consideration by pastors and members. Reasonable people may come to different conclusions about the best course of action. Some communities of faith appear to be better able than others to resolve differences and achieve positive outcomes.

When pastors described the conflict in their congregation over the past two years, about half said their church had experienced some minor

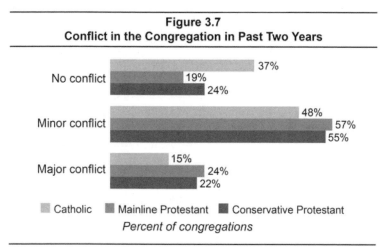

Figure 3.7
Conflict in the Congregation in Past Two Years

No conflict: 37%, 19%, 24%

Minor conflict: 48%, 57%, 55%

Major conflict: 15%, 24%, 22%

■ Catholic ■ Mainline Protestant ■ Conservative Protestant
Percent of congregations

conflict (see Figure 3.7). One in four pastors (23%) said their congregation had experienced major conflict in the past two years–with a few (14%) reporting that leaders or people had left as a result.

What was the conflict about? Pastors mentioned pastoral leadership style (31%) and finances (27%) most often. Other common issues include changes in the worship style (19%), a new building or renovations (18%), and other changes in congregational programs (15%).

How did the congregation handle the conflict? Many congregations use existing policies and procedures to resolve any differences that arise (43%). When conflict requires extraordinary means to resolve, leaders may hold a congregational meeting to discuss the issue (26%).

Pastor Profile

The Absolute Essentials in Small and Rural Churches

In a small, rural church, alone, with total responsibility on your shoulders, in the weekly treadmill of sermons and pastoral care, if you are not careful there is too little time to read and reflect, too little time to prepare your first sermons, so you develop bad habits of flying by the seat of your pants, taking short cuts . . . so you need to take charge of your time, prioritize your work, and be sure that you don't neglect the absolute essentials while you are doing the merely important. If you don't define your ministry on the basis of your theological commitments, the parish has a way of defining your ministry.

William H. Willimon, "Between Two Worlds" in *From Midterms to Ministry: Practical Theologians on Pastoral Beginnings*, ed. Allan Hugh Cole (Grand Rapids: Eerdmans, 2008), 284. Cf. 274–86.

How Are Congregations Strong?

Congregations are like snowflakes; no two are alike. Similarly, congregational vitality takes on many shades and shapes. In our previous research, we detailed ten important aspects of church health that make churches strong. By shifting the spotlight to the positives–what is going well in the faith community–congregations gain leverage for taking steps to build on existing strengths.

What are the strengths of successful congregations? Strong congregations (1) help their worshipers grow spiritually, (2) provide meaningful worship, (3) are places where worshipers participate in the congregation in many ways, (4) give worshipers a strong sense of belonging, (5) care for children and youth, (6) focus on the community, (7) help worshipers share their faith with others, (8) welcome new people, (9) rely on empowering congregational leadership, and (10) have a positive outlook on the future.[15]

In subsequent chapters, we summarize how these strengths play out in congregations with different types and styles of leaders. We answer this important question: What contributions do pastors make, over and above what worshipers bring, to the overall vitality of the congregation?

Ten Strengths of Congregations

- **Growing spiritually**. Where many worshipers are growing in their faith and feel the congregation meets their spiritual needs.
- **Providing meaningful worship**. Where many worshipers experience God's presence, joy, inspiration, and awe in worship services and feel worship helps them with everyday life.
- **Participating in the congregation**. Where many worshipers attend services weekly and are involved in the congregation in other ways.
- **Giving a sense of belonging**. Where many worshipers have a strong sense of belonging and say most of their closest friends attend the same congregation.
- **Caring for children and youth**. Where many worshipers are satisfied with the offerings for children and youth and have children living at home who also attend there.
- **Focusing on the community**. Where many worshipers are involved in social service or advocacy activities and work to make their community a better place to live.
- **Sharing faith**. Where many worshipers are involved in evangelism activities and invite friends or relatives to worship.
- **Welcoming new people**. Where many worshipers began attending in the past five years.
- **Empowering leadership**. Where many worshipers feel the congregation's leaders inspire others to action and take into account worshipers' ideas.
- **Looking to the future**. Where many worshipers feel committed to the congregation's vision and are excited about the congregation's future.

Location, Location, Location

Many considered St. Mary's Parish a plum appointment in the diocese—a beautiful location, many young families, and a talented lay staff. Yet Father John didn't anticipate how the big gap between his past parishes—all inner-city churches—and this new one in a suburban setting would come out in powerful ways. He took the advice from his mentor seriously: "Do not change anything in the first year. Just observe." But his desire to quickly shape the parish made that advice hard to follow. Shortly after his arrival, he announced that students would take their confirmation classes in the eleventh grade, a change from the current practice of enrolling eighth grade students. Father John failed to discuss this seemingly harmless change with Elizabeth, the director of religious education, other staff, or parish parents. Elizabeth and a dozen parents angrily demanded to meet with him. He was mystified by how such a minor adjustment in the education program could be read as the end of the world! During their tense meeting, Father John learned that in the suburbs, extensive after-school activities kept many 11th-grade students from participating in the parish's confirmation classes. He apologized to Elizabeth and the parents for not consulting with them and reversed his decision. Silently, he vowed not to make even the smallest change before discussions with staff and parishioners.

Finding a Fit in Place

Effective pastoral leaders participate in the community where they serve. They observe the ways the church's traditions intertwine with the community's fortune. Subsequent chapters document how features of the church and community—faith tradition, worship attendance, staffing, conflict, and geographic location—mesh with effective leadership patterns. In addition, we explore the linkages between congregational strength and pastoral leadership.

Questions for Pastors

- How does your current congregation compare with the churches you have previously served in terms of their size, resources, lay leadership, setting (urban, suburban, rural), region of the country, or theology? How do you see these factors shaping your ministry and leadership?
- What skills do you feel are most important for a pastor leading this type of congregation? How can you sharpen your skills in these areas?

Questions for Lay Leaders

- During the past five years, what are some of the best things that have happened in your church? What are some of the best things you see happening in your congregation right *now*?
- What are some of your hopes and dreams for your church's future?

REV PERCIVAL WAS LIVING THE DREAM...
SERVING GOD AND IMPERSONATING ELVIS.

Chapter 4

What Gives a Pastor Satisfaction in Ministry?

What brings pastors the greatest joy and satisfaction in their life and ministry? Pastors who believe that they are competent and possess a sense of accomplishment accrue positive feelings about their current ministry.[1] However, when individuals give more to their job than they receive, the imbalance between the positives and negatives can lead to stress, health issues, and eventually burnout. Tired, stressed, or burned-out pastors may wound the church's organizational and spiritual life as well. When stress or burnout grows severe, pastors may leave parish ministry for secular jobs or other ministry settings. Then congregations that need leadership lose their pastor's gifts and experience.

This chapter delves into the complex issues around the positive side of ministry–the many types and sources of pastors' satisfaction. We explore three areas of the pastoral experience: satisfaction with ministry, satisfaction with support for ministry, and satisfaction with personal life.[2] We also return to the church we introduced in Chapter 2. Now we'll see how hidden expectations about a pastor who actively participates in the community collide with Ted's lack of clarity about what brings him joy in ministry.

A Compromise Candidate: Pines Community Church

During the month of June, all three candidates visited with the pastoral search committee and provided a sermon podcast. Ted's time with the church leaders went well. They were impressed with his expertise in theological matters and emphasis on the Bible in preaching. He combined strong administrative skills with a highly spiritual and comforting approach to problem solving. Ted mentioned in their conversations that he felt called to serve as a military chaplain at some point. The church members could only be supportive of his call because they, too, saw themselves as patriotic. A few in the group expressed concern about Ted's quiet ways, but others read it as shyness or as a sign of spiritual depth. In the end, their opinions about the other two candidates divided the committee, but the majority felt comfortable with Ted. They believed he represented a good compromise and asked Ted to come serve as their new pastor.

Satisfaction with Ministry

How do pastors feel about their current ministry? Pastors' sense of effectiveness and their satisfaction with interpersonal church relationships are considered first.

Sense of overall effectiveness in ministry. Pastors' self-reports reveal their perception of how well things are going currently in their church. Only among Catholic priests are a majority "very satisfied" with their overall effectiveness as a leader in their parish (see Figure 4.1). In contrast, a majority of Protestant pastors say they are "somewhat satisfied" with their effectiveness in their current setting (52% of mainline and 64% of conservative Protestant pastors). Nonetheless, in all three groups very large majorities are either "very satisfied" or "somewhat satisfied" with their effectiveness (86% overall).

Satisfaction with work in ministry. Another survey item assessed the level of satisfaction pastors feel in general with their current work. Again, Catholic priests express greater satisfaction than Protestant pastors (two out of three priests say they are "very satisfied"). The majority of conservative Protestant pastors are only "somewhat satisfied" with their current ministry work (59%).

Satisfaction with lay relationships. A big part of a pastor's role involves working with the congregation's lay leadership. Sometimes those relationships go smoothly, while at other times they can be marked by conflict. Protestant pastors express higher satisfaction with this aspect of their ministry than the previous two elements. Yet again, Catholic priests exhibit the highest levels of satisfaction with their lay leader relationships.

In general, Catholic priests are the *most* satisfied with their ministry. Mainline Protestant pastors express more ministry satisfaction than

Figure 4.1: General satisfaction of pastoral leaders with ministry

	Catholic (%)	Mainline Protestant (%)	Conservative Protestant (%)
Overall effectiveness*			
Very satisfied	56	36	17
Your work in ministry*			
Very satisfied	67	44	36
Relationships with lay leaders*			
Very satisfied	56	50	43
Pastors with highest ministry satisfaction**	34	21	12

*Statistically significant difference among faith groups (p < .05).
**Pastors giving "very satisfied" responses on all three.

conservative Protestant pastors. Catholic priests say they are more satisfied with their overall effectiveness and current work in ministry than Protestant pastors. Only in the area of relationships with lay leaders are mainline Protestant pastors as satisfied as Catholic priests.[3]

Satisfaction with Support for Ministry

Denominational agencies and peers outside the congregation supply much-needed support for pastors. How do pastors assess that encouragement and backing?

Satisfaction with support from denominational officials. Pastors are somewhat less satisfied with the support they receive from their denominational officials than they are with other aspects of ministry. One third or fewer feel "very satisfied" with this type of help and support (see Figure 4.2).

Satisfaction with relationships with other clergy. Colleagues offer another possible source of continuing support for pastors as they carry out their ministry. Supportive relationships with other clergy provide a peer group whose members experience similar challenges. They might share ideas, resources, and other helpful tools. In general, pastors are less satisfied with the support they receive from their denominational officials and their peers than with their ministry overall.

Satisfaction with Personal Life

Given pastors' strong identification with their pastoral role, satisfaction with their ministry spills over into how they feel about their private life. Three measures appraise their satisfaction with elements of their lives apart from ministry.

Satisfaction with personal life. Pastors experience relatively high levels of satisfaction with their personal lives. There are no differences in personal life satisfaction among pastors in the three faith traditions (see Figure 4.3).

Satisfaction with relationships with family or friends. Protestant pastors and Catholic priests report about the same levels of satisfaction with family and friend relationships.

Satisfaction with life as a whole. Similar percentages of pastors, whatever their faith tradition, are "extremely delighted" with their life as whole.

However, the degree of personal life satisfaction Catholic priests and conservative Protestant pastors express falls short of their reports of general satisfaction with ministry. This is not the case for mainline Protestant pastors, whose self-reports of ministry and personal satisfaction are not significantly different.

Are Pastors Who Are Satisfied with Their Ministry also Satisfied with Their Personal Lives?

Yes! Pastors who are more satisfied with their current ministry are also more likely to be satisfied in their personal lives. Pastors who express higher satisfaction in their personal lives are more likely to be satisfied with their current ministry. Pastors who say they are satisfied with the level of support they receive from denominational officials and peers are more satisfied with their ministry and personal lives. Which comes first? That is unclear. Although we cannot assert that satisfaction in one area leads to satisfaction elsewhere, these three areas of satisfaction with ministry and life are strongly associated.[4]

What Lies behind Pastoral Satisfaction?

Now we turn to more detailed analyses of what lies behind pastoral satisfaction. In Chapter 2, we profiled pastors based on demographics,

---

Figure 4.2: Satisfaction with support for ministry

	Catholic (%)	Mainline Protestant (%)	Conservative Protestant (%)
Support from denominational officials			
Very satisfied	34	31	24
Relationships with other clergy			
Very satisfied	48	33	33
Pastors with highest satisfaction with support for ministry*	31	19	19

*Pastors giving "very satisfied" responses on both items. No items show a statistically significant difference at p < .05 across groups.

Figure 4.3: Personal life satisfaction*

	Catholic (%)	Mainline Protestant (%)	Conservative Protestant (%)
Personal life			
Very satisfied	48	40	47
Relationships with family/ friends			
Extremely delighted	29	23	28
Life as a whole			
Extremely delighted	36	25	36
Pastors with highest personal life satisfaction**	19	12	17

* Most other pastors chose the response option that was adjacent to the one shown (e.g., "satisfied" instead of "very satisfied").
** Pastors giving "very satisfied" or "extremely delighted" responses on all three. No items show a statistically significant difference at $p < .05$ across groups.

education, and experience. In Chapter 3, we focused on the many different types of congregations. Through statistical procedures, we separate out the relationship between these sets of factors and pastoral satisfaction. Which of them make a difference for pastors as they carry out their ministry?

Factors linked to satisfaction with ministry. Which pastors are the most satisfied with ministry in their current congregation? Our research shows that many factors lead to high satisfaction in ministry:

- **Female pastors.** Female pastors are more satisfied in their current ministry than male pastors.
- **Unmarried pastors.** Unmarried Protestant pastors express more satisfaction with their current ministry situation than married pastors.
- **More personal time.** Pastors who report spending more time socializing with their friends say they are more satisfied with ministry. On average, pastors report they devote two hours per week to social time with friends.
- **High satisfaction with spiritual life.** Pastors who say they are satisfied with their spiritual life are also more likely to feel satisfied in their ministry.
- **Sense of accomplishment and enthusiasm.** Pastors who have a sense of accomplishment in their ministry and feel enthusiastic about their work also affirm a greater sense of ministry satisfaction.
- **Satisfaction with salary and benefits.** While actual compensation levels are unconnected to satisfaction with ministry, pastors who are more satisfied with their salary and benefits are also more satisfied

with their ministry.

- **Lack of church conflict.** Pastors serving in congregations where there has been no conflict in recent years are more satisfied with their ministry than pastors serving in churches with minor or major conflict.

Factors linked to satisfaction with support for ministry. What group of pastors are the most satisfied with the support they receive from their denomination and other clergy? Our research shows that several factors are linked to high satisfaction with ministry support:

- **First ministry position.** Pastors who are serving in their first call are more satisfied with the external support they receive for their ministry than pastors who are beyond their first call. Many pastors in their first church position still have strong connections to seminary classmates who are also first-call pastors. Also, many have recently received denominational support in finding their first call. These factors may make them more keenly aware of the help they get from other clergy and denominational officials as they begin their ministry.
- **Larger share of time in preaching and worship leadership.** Pastors who report spending more time on preaching and worship leadership (including sermon preparation) are also more satisfied with the level of external support they receive. Those pastors who spend more time on interdenominational or interfaith activities also report higher levels of satisfaction with external support.[5]
- **Sense of accomplishment and enthusiasm.** Pastors with a strong sense of accomplishment in their ministry and those who are enthusiastic about their work also affirm greater satisfaction with the levels of external support they receive.
- **Satisfaction with salary and benefits.** Pastors who are more satisfied with their salary and benefits are also more satisfied with their sense of external support for ministry. Again, actual compensation levels are irrelevant to satisfaction with external support.
- **Single-vocation pastors.** Pastors who serve solely as church leaders are happier with the external support they receive from the denomination and other pastors. Tentmakers—those pastors who hold a secular job in addition to serving as a church leader—express less satisfaction with the support they receive for their ministry.
- **Presence of church conflict.** Pastors serving in congregations that are experiencing conflict are actually more satisfied with the level of external support than pastors in no-conflict situations. Perhaps pastors turn to colleagues and denominational officials when they are struggling to deal with difficult church issues.

Pastor Profile

More Time Needed for Sermon Preparation

My first pastorate was in a small Missouri town of 400. I think the other pastor in town had two books, the Bible (KJV) and a Webster's dictionary. Preaching at community services, he would read from the Bible and tell us what Webster said about various words in the text. I never cared for his preaching the dictionary and wished he had more books. At some point, he apparently got hold of another book. Unfortunately, it was a biography of Elvis, and the Easter Sunrise sermon was a comparison of the life, work, death and tomb of the King of Kings and the king of rock and roll. I gained a new appreciation for preaching the dictionary.

Charles V. Spencer, *Update: Stewardship, Mission Interpretation, Mission Funding Network,* Presbyterian Church (USA), Louisville, Ky., January 2000.

Factors linked to satisfaction with personal life. Many pastors find saving space in their lives for family, friends, recreation, and rest to be a continuing challenge. Some church leaders succeed at this more than others. What kinds of pastors find the greatest satisfaction in their personal life and with life as a whole?

- **More years in ministry.** The more years pastors have served in local church ministry, the more highly they rate their satisfaction with their personal life and life as a whole. Perhaps those pastors who were least happy left ministry early on or seasoned pastors find ways to obtain what they need for a happy private life.
- **Married pastors.** Married pastors find greater satisfaction in their personal life than single pastors. Time spent with their spouse and family seems to increase life satisfaction levels.
- **More personal time.** Pastors who spend more time working on hobbies or engaging in some form of recreation express higher levels of satisfaction with their personal life. Pursuing personal interests indicates that pastors have successfully carved out room for nonchurch activities even when the time spent is relatively modest (an average of two hours per week).
- **High satisfaction with spiritual life.** Pastors who are more satisfied with their spiritual life are also happier with their personal life.
- **Enthusiasm for ministry.** Pastors who remain enthusiastic about their work also report greater satisfaction with their personal life and life as a whole. Pastors who report higher levels of life satisfaction are also more likely to encourage others to enter ministry.

- **Lack of church conflict.** Pastors serving in congregations free from conflict are happier in their personal life and with life as a whole than pastors whose congregations face conflict.

When Unstated Assumptions Prevent a Good Match

Pines Community Church warmly welcomed Ted and his family. Church members hosted them in their homes and invited Ted to attend community events as their guest. After several months, members became aware that Ted's wife was homeschooling their children. They also observed that Ted rarely took part in activities outside the church. Although Ted got along well with church staff, he waited for members to approach him. Six months after his arrival, the personnel committee met with Ted and their dissatisfaction with these issues surprised him. Ted explained that as an introvert he tended not to seek out new people or activities. He countered their views that homeschooling his children sent a negative message to the community about local schools and that it closed down another avenue for him to connect with people outside the congregation. The meeting became even more tense when Ted diverted the discussion to his concerns about the church's shaky finances. He wondered aloud whether the budget could continue to support his full-time salary in the future. Both parties realized too late that they didn't get all the information they needed to make a good decision about the pastor-congregation match. Conflict was the result.

What Brings Pastors the Greatest Satisfaction?

For most pastors, Sunday is the highlight of their week. The opportunity to worship God in community with others forms the core of pastoral ministry. Yet, when Monday morning arrives, what brings their lives meaning and purpose that will sustain them until the next Sunday? In general, Catholic priests have a greater sense of satisfaction with their ministry than Protestant pastors, but they are not any more satisfied with their personal lives than Protestant pastors. Protestant pastors find joy in marriage, family life, and socializing with their friends. Catholic priests find similar joy in their connections to friends and family.

The presence of church conflict makes a huge difference in how pastors feel about their ministry, and church conflict is associated with lower levels of personal life satisfaction among pastors. Pastors who can remain enthusiastic about their work, feel a sense of accomplishment in their ministry, and nurture a strong spiritual life seem better able to buffer the impact of negative experiences.

Profile of Pastors Who Are Satisfied with Ministry

- Most pastors are highly satisfied; Catholic priests report the greatest satisfaction.
- Satisfaction is fueled by a sense of accomplishment, taking enough personal time, adequate compensation, and spending a greater share of time on preaching and worship leadership.
- Church conflict is detrimental to satisfaction with ministry.

Does the Size of the Church Matter?

On the surface, some might think that the size of the congregation–as measured by the average number of weekly worshipers–would be connected to satisfaction with ministry, current support for ministry, and personal life satisfaction. Are pastors serving in large churches more satisfied with their work in ministry, the support they receive, and their personal life? When we consider church size alongside other important facets connected to how pastors experience ministry, the effects of size melt away. Many other dimensions of the ministry experience and setting emerge as significant for understanding satisfaction with ministry, support, and personal life–as the lists above show–but size does not.

Other ministry aspects that could logically be linked to pastors' sense of satisfaction–when tested–actually appear on the "not important" side of the ledger. For example, the pastor's compensation, church location, time spent in a range of ministry activities, and ways personal time is spent are not important in predicting life and ministry satisfaction.

Pastors yearn for a ministry that matters. Those who serve in local churches believe that ministry is the best way they can serve God. Those pastors reaching the highest levels of ministry and life satisfaction do not doubt that belief.[6]

Questions for Pastors

- What one or two ministry tasks occupy the bulk of your time? What things do you find yourself doing that make you wonder whether they are a waste of time? ·
- Over the past several years, has there been any conflict in your congregation? What was the conflict about and how was it handled? What did church leaders and you learn from these experiences?

Questions for Lay Leaders

- Do you and other leaders want your pastor to motivate, organize, and equip you for ministries, or do you want a hired hand who takes the lead in all the ministries for you?
- Can your pastor have a new vision for the congregation, or will some of your worshipers interpret that new vision as an inappropriate agenda?

EVEN IN HIS WILDEST DREAMS,
REV. THOMAS HAD NEVER IMAGINED
SUCH A PERFECT MINISTRY OPPORTUNITY

Chapter 5

What Supports a Pastor's Well-Being?

The health of workers in any field impacts the organization where they work. Many argue that in the case of ministry these linkages are even more pronounced. Pastors try to be available when people require their help–not merely during nine-to-five office hours, but on weekends and at odd hours when emergencies arise. At the same time, people believe pastors draw on a deep well of spiritual resources. Worshipers trust that these assets protect pastors from stress. Yet pastors are human, and they are not immune to job stress and other negative experiences.

This chapter focuses on three dimensions of well-being: physical health, emotional health, and job stress. We also look at specific self-care mechanisms that some pastors use to deal with ministry pressures. Our purpose is to answer two questions: How healthy are today's pastors? How are physical health, subjective health, and emotional health related?

Off to a Good Start: Franklin Downtown Church

Chris accepted the congregation's call to serve as their pastor. His wife, Elena, a physician assistant, quickly found a position at the community clinic and their children adapted well to the church's day-care program. Chris and Elena regularly worked out separately during the week, but on Saturday they planned some kind of physical activity for the whole family. Chris had talked with the personnel committee about a plan for days off, vacations, office hours, and home/hospital visitations. Together they agreed that Friday afternoon and Saturday would be Chris's time off, unless an emergency arose. Chris planned to be in the church office Monday to Friday from 9:00 a.m. until noon. He would use the afternoons for study, community meetings, and visitation. With the church's permission, Chris contacted a retired pastor and asked him to serve as an unpaid parish associate. This parish associate would step in when Chris was out of town or unavailable. The many conversations Chris had with the search and personnel committees about his expectations and theirs made for smooth sailing in his first six months. Even pastors and churches enjoy a honeymoon period.

Physical Health

A pastor's physical health undergirds overall well-being. We looked at physical health in two ways: objectively and subjectively.

Objectively measured health. Body mass index (BMI), a widely used measure of body fat, is based on self-reported height and weight.[1] People with higher BMI scores (indicating they are overweight or obese) are at risk for many health risks including heart disease, type 2 diabetes, hypertension, and stroke. Unfortunately, only one quarter of pastors fall in the normal or underweight categories. In addition, more pastors than adults in the general population are overweight or obese (see Figure 5.1). Thus three in four pastors face weight-related issues. Among mainline Protestant

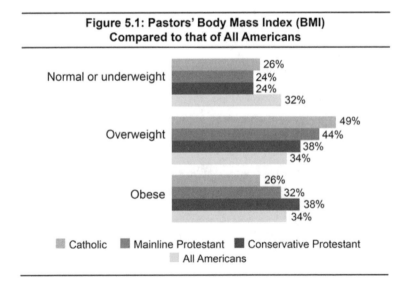

Figure 5.1: Pastors' Body Mass Index (BMI) Compared to that of All Americans

Normal or underweight
- 26%
- 24%
- 24%
- 32%

Overweight
- 49%
- 44%
- 38%
- 34%

Obese
- 26%
- 32%
- 38%
- 34%

Catholic   Mainline Protestant   Conservative Protestant   All Americans pastors–the only group in our sample with female pastors–obesity challenges more women (44%) than men (27%).

Self-reported physical health. *Physical health* forms the bedrock of overall well-being. People in poor health frequently lack the stamina and resilience to meet pastoral ministry requirements. We assess *physical health* and its impact on the pastor's work in four areas: self-described health, whether pain interfered with normal activities, whether physical health or emotional problems interfered with social activities, and satisfaction with health.[3]

In general, most pastors enjoy good health and face few problems due to their physical condition (see Figure 5.1). More Protestant pastors than Catholic priests describe their health as "excellent" or "good" and are "delighted" with their health. Both of these differences probably signal the older median age of Catholic priests.

Pastors with the best physical health give positive responses to all four questions (see last line in Figure 5.2). Only a minority of pastors achieve this high level of self-reported physical health. Rather, the majority of pastors can benefit from health improvements.

Emotional Health

A pastor's emotional health also contributes to overall well-being and depends in part on physical health. A variety of terms including *coping, depression,* and *exhaustion* describe emotional health.

Figure 5.2: Pastors' self-reported physical health

	Catholic (%)	Mainline Protestant (%)	Conservative Protestant (%)
Physical health is "excellent" or "very good"*	60	78	69
"Delighted" with their health* **	48	51	62
Pain interfered with normal activities "not at all" or "a little bit"	84	88	86
Physical/emotional problems interfered with social activities "none of the time" or "a little of the time"	84	89	87
Pastors with the best physical health***	35	41	43

*Statistically significant difference between pastors in different faith groups.
**Includes the first two response options on a seven-point scale labeled "delighted" at one end and "terrible" at the other.
***Pastors giving all four of the responses shown above.

Self-reported emotional health. Five questions measure self-reported *emotional health*: feeling calm and peaceful, having a lot of energy, feeling downhearted and depressed, feeling worn out, and feeling happy.[4]

Most pastors are generally happy, have a lot of energy, and feel calm and peaceful. Most are free from feelings of depression and weariness (see Figure 5.3). Many more Catholic priests than Protestant pastors feel calm and happy most of the time. More mainline Protestant pastors than others are free from exhaustion.

Pastors enjoying excellent emotional health answer each of the five questions with positive responses (see last line in Figure 5.3). Only a minority of pastors reaches this high level of self-reported emotional health. Many pastors risk the negative consequences of poor emotional health.

Stress and Its Impact on Well-Being

Job stress refers to the "harmful physical and emotional responses that occur when the requirements of the job do not match the capabilities, resources, or needs of the worker."[5] In ministry, this means the pastor suffers negative experiences due to insufficient resources, overwhelming demands, and other factors. People possess different tolerance levels for stress and differ in their resiliency in the face of trying situations. What is

Figure 5.3: Pastors' self-reported emotional health

	Catholic (%)	Mainline Protestant (%)	Conservative Protestant (%)
"All of the time" or "most of the time" in the past four weeks:			
Been happy*	94	75	78
Felt calm and peaceful*	78	54	66
Had a lot of energy	60	57	51
"None of the time" or "a little of the time" in the past four weeks:			
Felt downhearted and depressed	84	77	73
Felt worn out*	54	64	49
Pastors with excellent emotional health**	32	31	28

*Statistically significant difference between pastors in different faith groups.
**Pastors giving all five of the responses shown above.

stressful to one pastor might not be stressful to another. Stress can result in negative outcomes including job dissatisfaction, poor health, and exhaustion in ministry.

Two key elements related to job stress emerge from pastors' responses: job stress itself and ministry's interference with one's personal life. The latter results when pastoral responsibilities spill over beyond normal job boundaries and limit the pastor's ability to maintain a personal life.

Pastors' experiences with job stress. We assess job stress with eight questions (see Figure 5.4).[6] Of the eight items, the largest numbers of pastors experience these three: stress due to challenges in their congregation, feeling drained in fulfilling pastoral responsibilities, and being frustrated in accomplishing their work. (Responses of Catholic priests and mainline and conservative Protestant pastors do not differ. Figure 5.4 shows overall results.)

Almost four in ten pastors are free from stress (those who report they are not experiencing any of the eight facets of job-related stress; see last line in Figure 5.4). The remainder—a majority of pastors—suffer from at least one dimension of job stress and are at risk for related negative outcomes. Efforts to reduce stress would benefit most pastors in preventing physical and emotional health problems, exhaustion, and burnout. Taking such steps would also ensure they build the stamina to face pastoral demands.

Ministry role disrupting personal life. Interference with everyday life reveals the extent to which a pastor's ministry responsibilities disrupt other

---

Figure 5.4: Pastors' job stress

	All pastors (%)
Experienced stress due to challenges faced in the congregation "very often" or "often"	35
Are frustrated in accomplishing important tasks ("strongly agree" or "agree")	35
Feel drained in fulfilling functions in the congregation ("strongly agree" or "agree")	30
Have felt lonely and isolated "very often" or "often"	21
Are less patient with people in the congregation ("strongly agree" or "agree")	14
Experienced stress from dealing with members who are critical of the pastor "very often" or "often"	13
Experienced lack of agreement between congregation and pastor about the pastor's role is a "great problem" or "somewhat of a problem"	12
Feel negative or cynical about people in the congregation ("strongly agree" or "agree")	6
Pastors free from stress*	36

*Pastors giving none of the eight responses shown.

aspects of his or her life. We measure *interference* in three areas: difficulty having a private life, difficulty finding time for recreation or relaxation, and feeling that people in the congregation make too many demands.[7]

Looking across the three dimensions of *interference*, we find that majorities of Catholic and mainline Protestant pastors recount difficulty finding time for personal pursuits (see Figure 5.5).

One half of conservative Protestant pastors and about one third of mainline Protestant and Catholic leaders do not have trouble due to ministry–private life overlap (see last line in Figure 5.5). Yet substantial numbers report one or more ways in which their ministry interferes with their personal life. This suggests that pastors need to make efforts to (a) establish boundaries between ministry and private life and (b) regularly carve out time for personal pursuits. Self-care techniques (such as those described in the next section of this chapter) fit this bill.

Pastoral Self-Care

Some pastors take advantage of options to practice self-care such as prayer, sabbaticals, time off, or exercise. Engaging in self-care activities fosters health and prevents minor job-related stressors from ballooning into something more serious. Self-care assists pastors in maintaining their enthusiasm for ministry and staying fit to face ministry challenges. We review several self-care options and learn how common—or uncommon—each strategy is among pastoral leaders.[8]

Taking time off weekly. Regular time away from the job provides rest, reenergizes, and establishes clear boundaries between ministry and personal

Figure 5.5: Ministry's interference with everyday life

	Catholic (%)	Mainline Protestant (%)	Conservative Protestant (%)
Finding time for recreation, relaxation, or personal reflection is a "great problem" or "somewhat of a problem."*	59	61	40
Having a private life apart from one's ministerial role is a "great problem" or "somewhat of a problem."*	41	26	17
People in the congregation have made too many demands on you "very often" or "fairly often."	23	16	14
Pastors experiencing no interference**	34	35	56

*Statistically significant difference between pastors in different faith groups.
**Pastors giving none of the six responses shown.

time. Because pastors have major responsibilities on the Sabbath, taking another day of the week off fills that need for rest and restoration. Eight in ten pastors report that they regularly take one day off a week. More mainline Protestant pastors (87%) than Catholics (75%) and conservative Protestants (70%) regularly take a day off each week. Many pastors take either Fridays (44%) or Mondays (33%) off.

Finding personal time. Spending time in activities such as personal devotions, exercise, recreation, and socializing gives pastors a break from ministry's demands and recharges their batteries. Figure 5.6 shows how pastors spend their time away from the congregation. Protestant pastors–most of whom are married, and many of whom have children at home–devote countless nonwork hours to family life. In contrast, Catholic priests dedicate almost as much time to personal spiritual practices as Protestant pastors devote to their families. Watching television comes in second place for Protestants and in third place for Catholics. Time spent reading takes second place among Catholics. On average, pastors spend less than an hour each day exercising, pursuing hobbies or recreational activities, or socializing with friends.

Participating in pastoral support groups. Many pastors find support from other pastors–people who face similar issues in congregational ministry. Peer groups might comprise a group who graduated from the same seminary, local pastors serving the same community, those with comparable ministry interests (congregational revitalization or hunger-related ministries, for example), or pastors from one denomination. Ongoing clergy peer groups effectively offer support to pastors.[9]

Most pastors participate in some kind of group that supports their ministry or offers continuing education. Eight in ten pastors (80%) report meeting regularly with other ministers or pastoral leaders in a small group for continuing education and support over the previous five years. More mainline Protestant pastors (84%) than Catholic priests (78%) or conservative Protestant pastors (73%) participate in peer groups. On average, pastors' peer groups meet 12 times a year for about two hours each time. Many pastors report that their group focuses on sharing ideas and resources (61%), sharing personal concerns and struggles (51%), and theological reflection or Bible study (34%). Six in ten participating pastors (61%) believe their congregation has been positively affected by their peer group involvement.

Pursuing continuing education. Learning and personal growth through continuing education can bolster a pastor's ability to meet ministry demands and increase his or her sense of competence. In general, pastors do a good job of pursuing additional education and training. Most pastors (88%) devoted at least one day to continuing theological education in the previous year. More Catholic priests (94%) and mainline Protestant pastors (94%) than conservative Protestant pastors (75%) have done so. It is most common

Figure 5.6: Pastors' personal time

	Mean hours spent in past seven days			
	All pastors	Catholic	Mainline Protestant	Conservative Protestant
Family life (time spent on family activities including meals)*	13	4	14	13
Watching television	8	7	8	7
Prayer, meditation, Bible reading, and other spiritual disciplines*	6	11	4	5
Using the Internet*	5	4	5	6
Reading (other than for sermons or teaching)	5	8	3	5
E-mail and text messaging	4	4	4	4
Physical exercise for your health	4	4	4	4
Recreation and hobbies*	2	3	2	2
Socializing or eating out with friends*	3	4	3	3

*Statistically significant difference between pastors in different faith groups.

for pastors to devote *one or two days* yearly to continuing education (45%). Fewer engage in full-day continuing education more often.

Taking a sabbatical. An extended Sabbath period, or sabbatical, offers time for sustained rest, renewal, or extended study. Many congregations, denominations, and other groups support pastoral sabbaticals. Some pastors include a sabbatical when negotiating their terms of call. Relatively few pastors have enjoyed the time away that a sabbatical affords. Two in ten pastors (19%) have taken a sabbatical in the past ten years. Among those who did so, the median length was 90 days (25% took a sabbatical of 30 days or less; 10% enjoyed a sabbatical of 180 days or more).

Pastor Profile

A Balanced Life

A pastor starting a new church in a tornado-damaged area of Alabama expected to find challenges. Many people had lost everything. Even after a long day helping others salvage what they could, she waited to take out her garbage until she spotted a neighbor whom she hopes will be open to her. What seems like a 24-hour job is effortless to her: "I'm always thinking of ways to reach others," she said. "It's who I am, and I love it." The joy and satisfaction she experiences through her ministry far outweigh its demands.

What Lies behind a Pastor's Well-Being?

So far, this chapter reviews each element of well-being alone. We acknowledge the strong interplay among them and their relationships with other dimensions. What are the most important factors that predict these various subjective aspects of pastoral well-being?

Self-reported physical health. Ten factors emerge as strong predictors of positive physical health:[10]

- **Low BMI.** Pastors with lower BMI scores report better physical health. It should not be surprising that BMI, which measures body fat and often identifies those at risk for disease, is critical in predicting how healthy pastors report that they are.
- **Good emotional health.** Strong emotional health contributes to strong physical health. However, their close relationship reflects the "chicken and egg" problem. Does poor emotional health lead to poor physical health? Or does poor physical health lead to poor emotional health? Our research does not allow us to answer that question. Rather, it confirms the strong relationship between the two.[11]
- **First-career pastors.** Those pastors who report that ministry is their first career benefit from better physical health than those who came to ministry after a long-term prior career.
- **Fewer years in ordained ministry.** Pastors who have been in ministry relatively fewer years report higher levels of physical health. Those with more time in ministry are also older, so this factor signals the impact of age on physical health as well. Many prior studies have found that physical health declines with age—whether you are a pastor or a plumber or a president.
- **High satisfaction with ministry.** The more satisfied pastors are with their ministry the better their self-reported physical health.
- **Male pastors.** Compared to female pastors, males report that they

have better physical health. This finding supports many previous studies. Researchers attribute the gap in part to biological differences, with the acknowledgement that many other factors also contribute.

- **Marriage.** Married pastors experience better physical health than those who are not married. Considerable other research supports this finding. Regardless of occupation, married people enjoy better health than those who are not married. Previous research also shows that men get more health benefits from marriage than women do.[12]
- **Fewer hours worked.** Pastors who spend fewer hours per week in pastoral ministry have better physical health. (Note that part-time pastors who work fewer than 30 hours per week were excluded from this analysis.)
- **More time spent in leisure activities.** Spending more time in leisure activities including physical exercise, recreation, socializing, and family life predicts good physical health.
- **Satisfaction with spiritual life.** Pastors who are more satisfied with their spiritual life have better self-reported physical health.

Together these ten factors offer the strongest indicators of good physical health, with BMI–an objective measure of health–as the strongest predictor. Yet many other factors that we did not ask about on the survey undoubtedly contribute to physical vitality. We must not overlook personal practices such as smoking, alcohol or drug use, and healthy eating. Medical risks such as high cholesterol or triglyceride levels certainly belong on the list, as do current and previous diseases and injuries.

Some factors that we might think are important in fact do *not* help predict good self-reported physical health. Receiving health care benefits from the congregation or denomination, taking a day off each week, and satisfaction with salary and benefits, for example, play an insignificant role in pastors' physical health.

Self-reported emotional health. Eight factors help predict positive emotional health:

- **Limited interference of ministry with private life.** Pastors who are relatively free from problems related to the overlap between their ministry and personal roles enjoy better emotional health.
- **Good self-reported physical health.** As described above, strong physical health and strong emotional health go hand in hand.
- **Satisfaction with ministry.** Pastors who are more satisfied with their ministry have better emotional health.
- **Satisfaction with spirituality.** Good emotional health goes together with pastors' satisfaction with their spiritual life.
- **More hours worked.** Surprisingly, better emotional health is found among pastors who work more (not fewer) hours per week in ministry.

(Note that part-time pastors who work fewer than 30 hours per week were excluded from this analysis.)

- **Higher compensation levels.** Those pastors whose total compensation package (including both salary and housing) is higher than average report better emotional health than those who earn less.
- **Unmarried pastors.** Protestant pastors who are not married (either never married or now divorced or widowed) enjoy better emotional health than those who are married.

Superior physical health, satisfaction with ministry and spirituality, good boundaries between ministry and private life, and other factors show strong linkages with excellent emotional health. Interestingly, married pastors experience better physical health, but unmarried pastors enjoy better emotional health. Pastors seeking to avoid depression and exhaustion would do well to ensure they set aside time for personal pursuits outside of their pastoral work. Pastors need to find multiple ways to increase their satisfaction with ministry.

Yet our analyses show that some things people often believe contribute to emotional well-being actually have virtually no impact. Male and female pastors experience similar level of emotional health, as do pastors with children living at home and those without. Time spent in personal devotions and in leisure, congregational size and conflict, and the share of work hours devoted to administrative tasks are irrelevant to pastors' emotional well-being.

Keeping job stress low. Nine factors make a major contribution to keeping the amount of job stress pastors experience low:

- **Satisfaction with ministry.** Pastors who are more satisfied with their ministry report less stress from their congregational work.
- **Self-reported emotional health.** Good emotional health shows a strong relationship to pastoral ministry that is free from stress.
- **Ministry's interference with private life.** Pastors who experience few difficulties maintaining a personal life separate from ministry also experience less job stress.
- **Lack of conflict.** Serving in a congregation that has faced little or no conflict in recent years means low job stress levels for the pastor.

Profile of Pastoral Well-Being

- Many pastors are overweight or obese.
- Pastors report good physical and emotional health.
- Most pastors experience some job stress and difficulty finding time for a private life.

- Effective self-care practices include weekly time-off, personal time, ministry support or peer groups, continuing education, and sabbaticals.

Yet the variety on these dimensions is great. Some pastors successfully keep their weight down. Many effectively walk the tightrope between the demands of ministry and the need for time away from ministry. A few fail to take appropriate self-care measures, and the consequences can be severe—ill health, injury, disease, depression, or burnout.

- **Regular time off.** Job stress is lower for pastors who regularly take a day off each week.
- **Smaller congregations.** Pastors who serve in smaller congregations report less job stress than those serving in larger churches.
- **Serving one congregation.** Compared to pastors serving more than one congregation (including multipoint parishes and yoked churches), those serving in just one congregation face less job stress. The complexity and time requirements of multiple churches take their toll on pastors.
- **Poor physical health.** Surprisingly, poor self-reported physical health—not good physical health—is related to lower levels of job stress. It's possible that pastors who face severe health issues have purposely worked to reduce their job stress.

Other elements do not help predict job stress levels. Despite what some might expect, marital status, gender, children living at home, years in ministry, compensation levels and whether one's personal financial situation is improving or getting worse, and how pastors spend their work and leisure time are all unrelated to the stress that pastors experience.

Of the nine factors that strongly predict freedom from job stress, four make the most difference for pastors who wish to avoid job stress: satisfaction with ministry, good emotional health, limited difficulties from ministry's interference with personal time, and lack of congregational conflict. Pastors who are experiencing difficulties in any of these areas risk the frustration, loneliness, and other difficulties that make up job stress. Taking regular time off and staying healthy will help prevent these problems.

Limiting ministry's interference with daily life. Eight factors strongly predict the extent to which pastors are successful in maintaining a private life apart from ministry:

- **Good emotional health.** Pastors who report good emotional health also say that their ministry does not disrupt their private live.
- **Male pastors.** Male pastors have fewer difficulties maintaining a private life.

- **Married pastors.** Compared to single pastors, those who are married and enjoy the support of a spouse report fewer issues with ministry impinging on their personal life.
- **Fewer hours worked.** Pastors who are not workaholics–limiting the hours they work in congregational ministry–experience less overlap between ministry and personal time. (Note that part-time pastors who work fewer than 30 hours per week were excluded from this analysis.)
- **Smaller share of time in congregational administration.** Pastors who spend less time in congregational administration experience less overlap between ministry and private life than those whose time is heavily invested in administrative tasks.
- **Smaller share of time in congregational work.** Pastors who spend relatively less time leading and preparing for worship and counseling, training, and visiting worshipers are more successful in maintaining separation between ministry and their private life.
- **Regular time off.** Just as regular time off helps keep job stress low, a day off each week also assists pastors in preventing ministry tasks from expanding excessively into personal time.
- **Sabbatical.** Surprisingly, pastors who took a sabbatical in the past ten years report more interference of their ministry on their private life than pastors who have not had a sabbatical. It's possible that pastors who were experiencing considerable overlap between ministry and personal life sought sabbatical time off as a way to cope with such difficulties.
- **Lower compensation levels.** Pastors with lower than average total compensation in their current call report little conflict between ministry and personal responsibilities.
- **Lack of conflict.** Serving in a congregation that is relatively free from conflict goes hand in hand with good boundaries between ministry and personal life.

What pastoral characteristics and aspects of ministry do not influence separation of pastoral and private lives? While marital status is important, having children still at home is not. Likewise, time spent in personal prayer and Bible reading or leisure activities, congregational size, serving more than one church or serving as a tentmaker do not contribute to our ability to predict pastors' skill at maintaining a personal life separate from their ministry.

Good self-reported emotional health emerged as the strongest predictor of adequate boundaries between ministry and personal time. Beyond that, working fewer hours, taking time off, and devoting less ministry time to aspects of ministry that might not be as rewarding (e.g., administrative tasks) also make a contribution. Pastors with lower compensation packages may be better able than those paid more to limit the time they feel obligated to be "on call" for pastoral ministry.

Needed: Peer Support

"Chris is a really nice guy and I love his family, but I don't know if I can sit through another one of his sermons!" Others made similar remarks before the grumblings reached Marvin, who chaired the church board. Marvin insisted that Paul, chair of the personnel committee, deal with it—and quickly! Paul reluctantly asked Chris to meet with the personnel committee. Paul began the meeting with prayer before explaining to Chris that many members were unhappy with his sermons. Paul reassured Chris that the meeting's purpose was to give him sermon feedback and to support his response to worshipers' criticism. Paul asked each committee member to list three positive words or phrases to describe Chris's sermons and then to list phrases suggesting positive changes. Paul gathered the sheets and read the positive lists aloud. They described Chris's sermons as comforting, focused on current topics, and short. The suggestion list ran much longer—the sermons needed to be more coherent and thought provoking, more focused on the Bible, and more relevant to spiritual growth. Chris listened carefully and took the time to consider what he had heard; he did not want to answer defensively. When he finally spoke, he agreed that preaching was not one of his strengths. He admitted that as a first-time solo pastor he had not been ready for the rigor of weekly sermon preparation. Committee members stressed the congregation's long history of excellent preaching—a tradition they wanted to maintain. Paul suggested that Chris join a local pastors' group that meets weekly for lectionary study. Chris felt that support from his peers would be of great help—with this issue and others. Chris committed to take their suggestions to heart and spend more time each week in study, sermon preparation, and prayer. Committee members pledged to pray for Chris and his worship leadership. Everyone agreed to meet again in three months to assess progress.

How Healthy Are Today's Pastors?

Significant numbers of pastors experience obesity, poor self-reported physical or emotional health, job stress, or inadequate balance between ministry and personal life. The impact that these interrelated concepts have on clergy mirrors that experienced by other professionals. We'll explore some of the implications of poor physical and emotional health and job stress in the next chapter. Many denominations have begun to put a priority on pastors' health and well-being, acknowledging that healthy clergy are more effective clergy.[13] Congregational leaders, too, need to understand these issues. They are on the front lines, so to speak, perfectly placed to lobby for better compensation, benefits, and support for their pastor and to encourage self-care.

Pastors are both blessed and cursed by who they are and where they serve. The toll of aging and many years in ministry can be successfully managed, as many leaders demonstrate. Male pastors and married pastors experience greater well-being than women and those who are single. Leaders in denominations and congregations must acknowledge and address the unique experiences of women pastors–particularly those who are single or raising children alone. Many female pastors face additional challenges in balancing personal and congregational needs. Characteristics of the congregation where a pastor serves–size, presence or absence of conflict, pastoral demands, and compensation practices–make a difference, too. Self-care, support from family and friends, and encouragement from lay leaders also influence how pastors sustain a healthy life and a healthy ministry.

Questions for Pastors

- How often in the past two years has poor physical health, emotional problems, or family demands interfered with your ministry effectiveness? How do you cope in such situations?
- What practices do you regularly engage in that sustain you physically, emotionally, and spiritually? Are additional efforts needed to support your well-being and reduce stress?
- If married, how would your spouse answer these questions?

Questions for Lay Leaders

- How often does the congregation make unreasonable demands on your pastor? How often are members and leaders unreasonably critical of your pastor? What steps could be taken to limit excessive demands and criticism?
- In what ways does the congregation show acceptance for your pastor? In what ways do you make your pastor feel loved and cared for?

Chapter 6

What Difference Do Satisfaction and Well-Being Make?

What are the implications of pastoral satisfaction and well-being? This chapter delves into how satisfaction and good health, on the one hand, and dissatisfaction and poor health, on the other, affect the pastor and, in turn, the congregation. In Chapter 4 we examined factors that contribute to a pastor's satisfaction with his or her ministry. Chapter 5 focused on the things that influence pastoral well-being. While satisfaction and well-being are themselves worthwhile goals, they also make a big difference in congregational life. Pastors who are satisfied with their ministry pour themselves into their congregations. Pastors who are dissatisfied with their ministry, on the other hand, may believe that a career change will improve the situation.

Change Happens: St. Mary's Catholic Parish

After reviewing the parish finances, Father John knew that their dwindling funds would not continue to support existing programs or subsidize new mission efforts. He did not know how he could improve their financial situation without casting himself as "the new priest who only talks about money!" Working with the finance council, Father John looked for ways to trim expenditures that would have a minor impact on current parish programs. He also asked the finance council to consider creative ways to increase revenue flow: Were community groups charged sufficiently for facility use, enough to cover the utility and maintenance costs? Did the parish conduct an annual steward-ship campaign? Father John also took the opportunity to discuss with families new to the parish regular church giving as a spiritual discipline. Fortunately, over time these multiple strategies brought the parish balance sheet into greater alignment with the new vision that Father John was casting for the parish. Longtime members noticed the long hours that he worked. His full-steam ahead, active leader-ship style stood in bold contrast to their former priest's laissez-faire style. Despite the mountain of work in this resurrecting parish, Father John fit the description of priests as "the happiest men in America."[1]

Signs of Impact

What signs of success or problems might indicate how satisfaction and well-being affect the pastor and his or her congregation? Our survey asked pastors to evaluate their ministry in both positive and negative ways.

Positive reflections on ministry. Almost all pastors (93%) report enthusiasm for their work. In fact, six in ten (59%) strongly agree with the statement "I have enthusiasm for my work." Similarly, nine in ten pastors (87%) believe they have accomplished many worthwhile things in their current church ministry, with one third (34%) *strongly agreeing* with the statement "I have accomplished many worthwhile things in my ministry here." We noted earlier that both enthusiasm for work and having a sense of accomplishment are linked to a pastor's satisfaction with ministry (which encompasses satisfaction with work in ministry, lay leaders in the congrega-tion, and one's effectiveness).

Negative reflections on ministry. Four survey questions asked about potential career changes ranging from finding another congregation to leaving ministry altogether (see Figure 6.1). Mirroring the positive findings for enthusiasm and a sense of accomplishment, the encouraging news sug-gests that few pastors have given serious thought in the past year to career changes. Of the four possible changes, more pastors considered leaving their current congregation (nonetheless, only 11%) than have thought about larger life-changing career moves. Fewer Catholic priests than Protestant pastors contemplated each potential option.

Pondering a career change often results from dissatisfaction with one's current position and burnout. Making a change allows escape from the things causing difficulties. Research shows that intentions are the best indicator of future action.[2] Looking closely at pastors who say they have seriously considered career changes gives us insight into potential turnover among congregational leaders.

Figure 6.1: Negative reflections on one's ministry

In past year, very often or fairly often	Catholic (%)	Mainline Protestant (%)	Conservative Protestant (%)
Seriously thought of leaving your current position to become a pastor elsewhere*	2	11	12
Seriously thought of leaving pastoral ministry in a church to take another type of ministry position*	2	10	9
Seriously thought of leaving pastoral ministry to enter a secular occupation*	4	5	10
Doubted that you are called by God to ministry*	0	2	8

*Statistically significant difference between faith groups (p < .05).

What Contributes to Pastors' Positive Reflections on Their Ministry?

All congregations benefit from leaders who find joy in ministry. Pastors remain committed to the congregation when they believe their ministry makes a difference. Here we identify the things that contribute to pastors' positive reflections on their ministry.

Factors linked to pastors' enthusiasm and a sense of accomplishment. What contributes to pastors' enthusiasm for their work *and* their sense of accomplishment? Four important predictors for *both* positive reflections on ministry surfaced:

- **Serving longer at their current church.** Pastors who are new to their position are still learning their way. As pastors settle in, enthusiasm for their work there grows; they begin to see the impact of their ministry.
- **Working more hours per week.** Pastors who work more hours each week evaluate their ministry more positively.
- **Lower satisfaction with salary and benefits.** Pastors who are less satisfied with their salary and benefits give more positive feedback about their ministry. Cognitive dissonance may come into play here: "If I'm not here for an excellent compensation package, then I must be here because I know my ministry is making a difference."[3]
- **Higher satisfaction with ministry.** Satisfaction with ministry goes hand in hand with enthusiasm and a sense of accomplishment.

Factors linked to pastors' sense of accomplishment but not their enthusiasm. These facets help to predict pastors' sense of accomplishing worthwhile things but are unimportant in understanding pastors' enthusiasm for their work:

- **Regularly taking a day off each week.** Those who enjoy a break from ministry each week feel they have accomplished more. The downtime that a day off provides may help recharge pastors for the coming week.
- **More time spent on administrative tasks.** Addressing the congregation's business side helps pastors feel they've accomplished valuable things.
- **Serving a church in a rural location.** Pastors in rural locations report they have accomplished more in ministry than those serving elsewhere. Addressing the challenges that rural ministry presents ensures pastors know they've achieved something worthwhile.

Factors linked to pastors' enthusiasm but not their sense of accomplishment. Some questions predict pastors' enthusiasm for pastoral ministry but show no relationship to their sense of accomplishment:

- **Serving in their first call.** Pastors who are just starting their ministry career have more enthusiasm for their work than those who have served other congregations previously.
- **Better emotional health.** Good emotional health predicts pastors' enthusiasm for their work.
- **Spending more time in leisure activities.** Pastors who devote more time to recreation and leisure activities outside the congregation remain more enthusiastic about their ministry.
- **Having children at home.** Pastors with children living at home express more enthusiasm for their work. Could it be that the joy and excitement that children bring carries over to ministry?

Unimportant factors. Many pastor characteristics (including gender and marital status), call characteristics (such as total compensation), and well-being measures (e.g., physical health) *do not* have an impact on pastors' sense of accomplishment or their enthusiasm for pastoral work.

Pastor Profile

Leaving Parish Ministry

Six months after she left her ministry at Immanuel Church, Joyce realized how terribly exhausted she had been. "I'm not sure I did a very good job there," she says. "I was tap-dancing all the time, trying to keep ministry alive and bring people along. But their sense of ownership wasn't really there." Now serving in a national denominational post, she's clear that if she returns to the parish, she'll do things differently. "I would not say, 'Let's do this. Come on, I'll show you how.' Instead, I would focus on helping folks discover their own sense of ministry. . . . It would be their impetus, not mine."

One of seven pastors profiled in Paul E. Hopkins, *Pursuing Pastoral Excellence* (Herndon, Va: Alban, 2011), 29.

What Contributes to Pastors' Negative Reflections on Their Ministry?

Pastors who feel their ministry is not going well may consider alternative calls. In this section we focus on the types of pastors, congregational settings, and ministry experiences that contribute to thoughts of leaving a congregation.

Factors linked to considering career changes. Whether a pastor leaves for another congregation, for other ministry, or for a secular position is irrelevant for congregational leaders. The impact is the same—"Our pastor left." Thus we focus here on the pastor's departure from his or her current congregation as the most important indicator. These aspects predict whether pastors contemplate making a career change:

- **Serving a smaller congregation.** Pastors serving in smaller churches are more likely to think about moving to a new congregation. Small congregations often face financial and other challenges that can make ministry difficult. Also, some pastors believe that being successful means serving in a larger church.
- **Serving a church in a rural location.** Rural churches, like small churches, can be difficult. Pastors serving in such locations are more likely to think about moving elsewhere. Some may feel personally isolated. Others may seek a change to improve their spouse's employment options or to broaden the educational possibilities available for their children.
- **Serving longer at their current church.** The longer a pastor has served a particular congregation the more frequent are his or her thoughts about moving to a new congregation. A pastor who stays for decades in the same congregation is relatively rare.
- **Lower satisfaction with ministry.** Pastors who are less satisfied with their ministry are more likely to consider seeking a new call. (See additional comments about job stress and satisfaction with ministry in the next section.)
- **Lower satisfaction with salary and benefits.** Similarly, dissatisfaction with compensation and benefits goes hand in hand with thinking about a new call. Actual compensation levels, though, are not related.

- **Higher satisfaction with spiritual life.** Pastors who focus on meeting their personal spirituality needs are more likely to consider leaving their current congregation.
- **More job stress.** Job stress is a clear predictor of contemplating departure. (See additional comments about job stress and satisfaction with ministry in the next section.)

Unimportant factors. As we discovered for pastors' positive reflections on ministry, many dynamics are unrelated to pastors' thoughts of leaving their current congregation. These include demographic characteristics (e.g., gender and marital status), call characteristics (e.g., hours worked per week), and their well-being.[4]

Outcomes of Pastoral Satisfaction and Well-Being

- Most pastors are enthusiastic about their ministry and feel they've accomplished a lot.
- First-call pastors, those with more years in their current church, and those most satisfied with ministry are most enthusiastic.
- One in ten considered leaving the congregation in the past year.
- Pastorates in small or rural churches prompt more thoughts about career change.
- High ministry satisfaction buffers high job stress and prevents burnout.

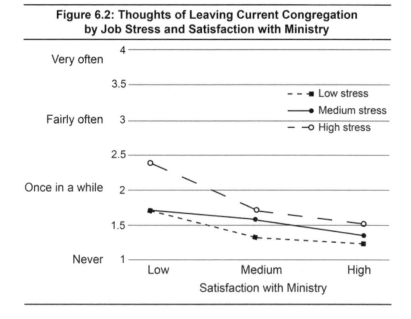

Figure 6.2: Thoughts of Leaving Current Congregation by Job Stress and Satisfaction with Ministry

Avoiding Burnout by Balancing Satisfaction and Stress

Many people believe that high stress levels cause burnout and drive pastors away from ministry. We found that satisfaction with ministry can offset the job pressures that pastors experience. Pastors reporting the highest satisfaction with their current ministry rarely thought about leaving their current congregation *regardless of their stress level.* (See Figure 6.2; the three points to the right–those who are most satisfied–are very close together.) The sense that their ministry is going well makes these pastors able to tolerate higher stress levels. Ministry satisfaction buffers them from difficulties they experience.

At the other extreme, pastors who are relatively dissatisfied with ministry *and* experience more job-related stress are those *most* likely to think about leaving their church (see the highest data point to the left for those with low satisfaction). For these pastors, high stress levels are out of balance with satisfaction, which is relatively low. This imbalance results in burnout, which leads pastors to consider career changes.[5]

Considerable previous research shows that job dissatisfaction is an excellent predictor of intent to leave a position. However, our findings reveal that it is more than dissatisfaction alone. Rather, *dissatisfaction tied with job stress* puts pastors at risk for leaving their congregation. In turn, their congregation risks the distractions and complications involved in searching for a new pastor, which can compromise its vitality.[6]

What Should Pastors and Congregations Understand about Satisfaction and Well-Being?

Father John's developing business sense proved critical for the parish's survival. Although his contribution went unnoticed by most parishioners, the lay staff expressed their appreciation and felt relief from constant money pressures. Father John also adjusted to the day-to-day grind of decision making. Almost all parish decisions arrived at his desk sooner or later, stretching his time-management skills. An unexpected struggle emerged. After years of theological study, he wanted to use what he had learned to change the world and his parish. But in the daily life of a parish, he found that honoring relationships often trumped his sense of mission urgency. He had not expected to experience so much conflict in God's service among God's people. Even prayerful and well-informed decisions sometimes yielded parishioner complaints. He came to realize that every parish has a small number of disgruntled people. An older colleague reassured him: "It doesn't matter whether you're serving a church of 60, 600, or 6,000. There will always be six people who drive you crazy."

The findings presented in this chapter offer clear implications for pastors and congregations. Satisfaction with ministry influences pastors' reflections on their ministry—both positive and negative. Pastors who are dissatisfied with their work in ministry *and* experience ministry-related difficulties are departures waiting to happen. Congregational leaders should be sensitive to the responsibilities they ask their pastor to meet. Providing the pastor with regular time away from the congregation, encouraging the pastor to take steps toward self-care, and limiting the pastor's workload all help to combat stress.

Pastors who enjoy their ministry and nurture strong relationships with lay leaders see good results. These pastors feel effective and remain enthusiastic about serving their current congregation. Indeed, every congregation and every pastor wants to achieve this goal.

Questions for Pastors

- Is there something that you're doing in your current congregation that you shouldn't be doing? Is this responsibility a wasted effort or an opportunity for someone else to be involved in ministry?
- Do you allow a few vocal people who resist change to derail the congregation's future? Can you listen courteously, pray for them, and respond wisely—yet resist their efforts to stop positive change?

Questions for Lay Leaders

- Do you publicly support the pastor and other leaders during times of substantial change?
- Are you doing all you can to contribute to your church's ministry? How can you step up as a partner in your congregation's ministries?

Chapter 7

What Part Do Pastors Play in Growing Congregations?

Defining church vitality is like defining love; there are thousands of metaphors, but none are completely descriptive. Numerical growth, one indicator of church vitality, has captured the attention of more researchers than any other topic about congregational life. At a minimum, church growth ensures the organization's survival. However, we do not believe that numerical growth is the only church health measure. Faith tradition and theology often dictate whether increasing worship attendance and adding members are seen as what God requires of a vital faith community. Some congregations place equal or greater emphasis on caring for current worshipers, community service and advocacy, or outstanding worship as their primary expressions of faithfulness. This chapter focuses on pastors and what they bring to the church growth equation. Is there anything about the pastor that is relevant to whether a church grows or not?

A Growing Pastor: A Growing Church

After 12 years, Franklin Downtown Church continues to grow under Pastor Chris's leadership. His preaching improved dramatically in his first year. In fact, his rapid progress led one church member to claim her prayers made Pastor Chris into a great preacher! Chris engaged in intentional practices to sharpen his sermon preparation and worship leadership. He received feedback on sermon topics and learned about helpful sermon resources from a weekly pastors' Bible study group. In addition, Chris invited a small group of thoughtful members to meet with him twice a month. In these intimate conversations, Chris discussed his sermon ideas, listened as members described their spiritual questions or needs, and took note of how they saw God working in their daily lives. Often Chris was able to use these insights to prepare his sermons. Worshipers began to comment favorably on the relevance of his sermons to their own spiritual struggles. Chris poured his energy into raising the bar on worship service quality. Through his wife, he became friends with the dean of the local university's music school. Chris recruited the school's graduate students to assist with music leadership during services. The church and music school formed a creative partnership to provide instrumental music lessons to neighborhood children. These efforts paid off. In his first eight years there, worship attendance climbed from 225 to almost 400, maxing out the sanctuary seating. Church leaders responded by organizing a second worship service with a more relaxed format. More than 100 people attended the first new service.

What Is Church Growth?

To identify growing churches, we examined their reported average worship attendance over the previous five-year period. Average worship attendance–rather than membership–gives a more valid indication of changes in participation for two reasons. First, denominations and faith groups use different church membership definitions. Second, many members do not regularly participate or attend services. In fact, typically worship attendance is about 50% of the congregation's membership.[1]

As we noted earlier (see Figure 3.3), over a five-year period, half of the surveyed congregations declined in worship attendance by more than 5%. We placed these congregations in the numerically *declining* category. We designated those congregations that reported that their average worship attendance grew by more than 5% as numerically *growing* churches. The remaining congregations fell in the *stable* category–neither growing nor declining by more than 5% over the same five-year period.[2]

What Lies behind Church Growth?

Congregations consist of particular people gathered for worship in a specific geographic location. Any understanding of church growth must take into account what is inside the congregation–the characteristics of the people who gather and the organization's features, such as its size and faith tradition. What is outside the congregation's doors, including the type of community where the church is located and the people who live there, matters too. Here, we add another important ingredient: what do we know about the pastor who leads a growing congregation?[3]

Who Worships in Growing Churches?

Before turning to pastors' role in church growth, we first consider the kinds of worshipers in growing churches and what they find valuable about their church.

- **Younger worshipers.** Growing churches draw younger worshipers than other churches: more people under the age of 45 and fewer who are 65 or older. The differences between growing, stable, and declining congregations shown in Figure 7.1 do not appear large. Yet the numbers represent the median percentage across all congregations in each age group. The most striking differences lie between growing and stable churches on the one hand (where typically one out of three worshipers is 65 or older) and declining churches on the other (where on average 41% of worshipers are 65 or older).

Figure 7.1: Age of worshipers in growing, stable, and declining churches*

Median percentage	Growing (%)	Stable (%)	Declining (%)
24 years or younger	7	5	7
25–44 years old	21	21	16
45–64 years old	40	40	36
65 years or older	33	35	41

*Statistically significant difference among the three groups. Median percentages for each worshiper age group are calculated from aggregated worshiper responses for individual churches.

- **People with a strong sense of belonging.** Much of congregational life revolves around the closeness people feel as they worship together, experience life's joys and sorrows, and share their deepest beliefs. Congregations that provide people with love, a sense of belonging, and self-esteem will attract and retain new members. Because growing congregations encourage emotional attachment, more of their worshipers feel a strong sense of belonging. Substantially lower percentages of worshipers in stable and declining churches report strong emotional attachments to the congregation.
- **Many new worshipers.** Congregations grow by bringing in more new people than they lose. Most congregations lose at least a few worshipers each year: some die, others move away, and sometimes people drift away and stop coming. If a congregation wants to grow

numerically, it must bring in more new people than are lost through attrition or death. In the average congregation, one in four people began attending in the past five years. Among growing churches, however, the median percentage of new worshipers exceeds that national average. One in *three* worshipers in growing churches came in the past five years. Because this percentage reflects the median, or middle score, half of growing congregations are welcoming even higher percentages of new people. These new worshipers are more than numbers. They bring new perspectives, energy, resources, and talent to the congregation.

- **Different types of new people.** *Transfers*–people who came from other congregations of the same denomination–are the largest group of newcomers across all churches. In declining churches, about half of new worshipers (46%) come as transfers. However, growing and stable churches draw in fewer transfers than declining churches. In contrast, growing churches attract three times more *first-timers*–those who have never attended anywhere–than declining churches (see Figure 7.2).

- **People strongly focused on the church's future.** Congregations thrive when a vision of what they *can do* drives their mission. They refuse to allow past or present circumstances to control their dreams. Superfocused on their future, these congregations attract committed worshipers who are excited about their involvement. Growing congregations include higher percentages of worshipers who place their bet on a hope-filled tomorrow than stable or declining churches.

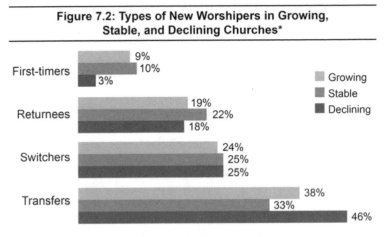

Figure 7.2: Types of New Worshipers in Growing, Stable, and Declining Churches*

First-timers: 9% / 10% / 3%
Returnees: 19% / 22% / 18%
Switchers: 24% / 25% / 25%
Transfers: 38% / 33% / 46%

Growing
Stable
Declining

Median percent of new people

*NOTE: New worshipers are those attending the congregation for five years or less. Median percentages for each type of new worshipers are calculated from aggregated worshiper responses for individual churches. Percentages will not total 100%.

Organizational Dynamics: What about Size, Theology, or Location?

Now we turn to organizational dynamics that relate to numerical growth: church size and theological orientation. We also target another important dimension that operates outside the congregation's direct control—the church's geographic location.

Size of the congregation. While other organizational aspects are stronger predictors of growth, church size does play a small role. Larger churches are more likely to report that they have grown. Why might that be? First, larger churches make a bigger target for those seeking a new church; they are easier to find. Second, larger churches typically offer more ministries and programs, meet in more modern facilities, and host an electronic presence (such as an appealing Web site). Combined, these characteristics make large churches a powerful draw for potential worshipers.

Recent studies document churchgoers' increasing concentration within very large churches—often, nondenominational Protestant churches.[4] However, larger churches face challenges not experienced by smaller churches—for example, more "free riders." Just like people who use public transportation without paying the fare, some worshipers take advantage of the church's programs without investing their time or money in return.[5] Larger churches also must address higher attrition rates and create innovative avenues for assimilating the many newcomers.[6]

Faith tradition or theology. Roughly equal percentages of congregations (about half) grow in all three faith groups. We found no statistically significant difference for growth among the three faith traditions included in our analyses. However, the factors behind church growth vary by the church's faith tradition. In other words, the things that fuel Catholic parish growth differ from what makes a mainline Protestant or conservative Protestant church attractive to new worshipers. For example, geographically defined Catholic parishes often experience growth from the influx of new immigrants who are already Catholic.

Another drum that scholars beat regarding church growth relates to theological orientation. The conservative-liberal theological continuum runs within all faith traditions. Some mainline Protestant churches attract members and leaders with liberal views, while other churches in the same denomination attract worshipers who hold a conservative orientation. Some argue that theologically conservative congregations are more likely to grow.[7] Others argue as loudly that more theologically liberal congregations are growing.[8] Our empirical research reveals little or no evidence that this single factor influences numerical growth.

Church growth is complex. Any religious leader or consultant who plays a "trump card"—focusing on *one* key factor that he or she believes causes growth or church vitality—plays with a losing hand. Theological orientation simply does not matter as much as some wish to believe. If we scale back the theology lens, perhaps congregational leaders can concentrate on what matters: Does the congregation's ministry focus fit its strengths and the community's needs?

Location, location, location. Congregations take on views and ways of explaining reality that relate to their geographic location.[9] A congregation's location script helps answer essential questions: Who are we? What is our mission in this place? As part of that script, many worshipers and leaders assume that location determines whether the church can grow or not.

As Figure 7.3 shows, in any kind of setting—a rural area, small town, suburb, or large city—some churches find ways to grow. Generally, growth happens in nonmetropolitan areas. Few growing churches (7%) are located in large metro areas. Growth is more common among churches in suburban areas—where one in three growing churches is located—compared to stable churches (5% in suburbs) or declining churches (18% in suburbs).

We found more stable and declining churches in rural areas and towns or small cities. This results from the larger population declines in rural areas and small towns than in suburbs and larger cities. As a result, churches in rural areas and towns struggle to attract enough new worshipers to replace the numbers of worshipers who move away or die.

What percentage of churches in rural areas are growing? Figure 7.3 does not answer this question; it shows that one in four growing churches is located in a rural area. However, around 17% of churches in rural areas, 17% of town/small city churches, 39% of suburban churches, and only 11% of large metropolitan area churches reported growth.

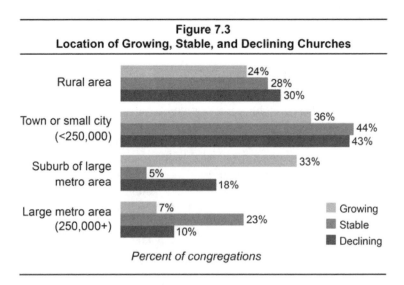

Figure 7.3
Location of Growing, Stable, and Declining Churches

Rural area: 24%, 28%, 30%
Town or small city (<250,000): 36%, 44%, 43%
Suburb of large metro area: 33%, 5%, 18%
Large metro area (250,000+): 7%, 23%, 10%

Growing / Stable / Declining

Percent of congregations

Profile of Growing Churches

- They represent one in four congregations
- Have fewer worshipers older than 65
- Attract many new worshipers, staying ahead of departures and deaths
- Attract more of the unchurched or first-time worshipers
- Offer an engaging vision for the future
- Are more often led by first-career or lifelong pastors
- Experience some conflict

Who Are the Pastors in Growing Churches?

Our research makes a unique contribution to unraveling growth dynamics because we add information about the pastors serving in growing, stable, and declining congregations. What do we know about the types of pastors and leadership patterns associated with growth?

Not young or old. A common assumption is that younger pastors, who often have the most energy and ambition, serve in growing churches. They either grow the church themselves or are called to a congregation that is already growing and wishes to continue that momentum. As Figure 7.4 shows, however, pastors between 51 and 60 years old are more common among growing churches than pastors in other age groups. More pastors older than 60 serve in declining churches. The majority of pastors in declining churches are over age 50.

Only 12% of pastors are 40 years old or younger. What percentage of that group serves in growing churches? One in four (26%) leads a growing church. Fewer pastors in the 41-to-50 age group (18%) lead a growing

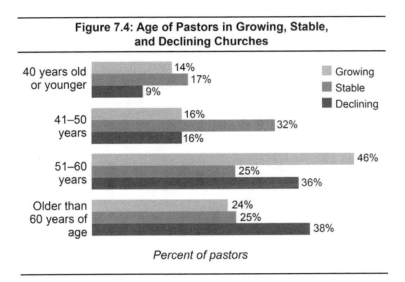

Figure 7.4: Age of Pastors in Growing, Stable, and Declining Churches

Percent of pastors

church. Almost one in three pastors between 51 and 60 years of age (30%) serves a growing a church. Finally, only 17% of pastors older than 60 lead a growing church.

First-career and lifelong pastors. Second-career pastors–those who worked in another occupation before entering ministry–represent 40% of pastoral leaders. These second-career leaders are overrepresented in declining churches (see Figure 7.5). This does not indicate that these pastors caused numerical decline. Rather, growing congregations may prefer first-career pastors and call them as leaders, if all else is equal. Growing and stable churches have more first-career pastors (64%) compared to second-career pastors (only 36%).

Some pastors leave parish ministry for a time to work in another setting (such as hospital chaplaincy) or find secular employment. All the pastors in our survey were *currently* serving in a local congregation, even if employment elsewhere previously interrupted their time in parish ministry. Some pastors have remained in local church ministry throughout their employment history–these are lifelong parish pastors. Higher percentages of growing churches are led by pastors in this second group, those spending their entire career in parish ministry, than stable or declining churches. Again, when growing congregations consider all the desired qualities and qualifications of pastors, they often seek leaders with uninterrupted experience.

What about female pastors and growth?

Only 28% of mainline Protestant pastors are women. However, they are overrepresented in growing churches—almost two in five growing-church pastors are female.

Pastors with longer service in their current church. The number of years a pastor serves a church shows an interesting relationship to numerical growth. Pastors in growing and declining churches have served those congregations

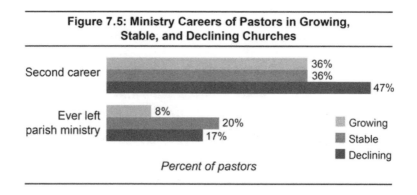

Figure 7.5: Ministry Careers of Pastors in Growing, Stable, and Declining Churches

longer, on average, than leaders in stable churches. To help a church grow takes time—to build trust, develop realistic strategies, and achieve results. Perhaps the longer service for declining church pastors reflects that they have stayed too long and are no longer effective in that church setting (see Figure 7.6).

Deals with church conflict. Most pastors deal with conflict over finances, church programs, worship service changes, and leadership styles at some point in their ministry. Around half of all congregations (56%) went through some *minor* conflict in the past two years. Because growing congregations employ diverse outreach strategies and face growth-related issues, it is likely that not everyone agrees about the best way forward. In fact, 70% of growing-church leaders report the congregation experienced minor conflict, compared to 42% of declining-church pastors.

Pastors with high enthusiasm and sense of accomplishment. As pastors in growing churches see tangible outcomes of their leadership, they feel more enthusiasm for ministry. Leading in a growing church also goes hand in hand with a greater sense of accomplishment.

Pastors expressing low satisfaction with their spirituality. The opposite trend appears with regard to satisfaction with one's personal spiritual life. As the percentage of growth increases, pastors report less satisfaction in this area. Perhaps pastors in declining congregations have more discretionary time for prayer and devotional study.

Unimportant factors. Many pastor characteristics (including marital status and theology), call characteristics (such as time spent in various pastoral responsibilities), and well-being measures (for example, physical and emotional health) are not relevant to church growth.

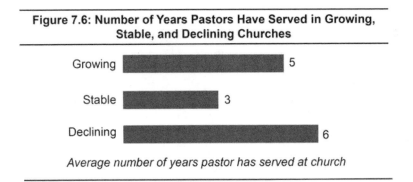

Figure 7.6: Number of Years Pastors Have Served in Growing, Stable, and Declining Churches

Growing 5

Stable 3

Declining 6

Average number of years pastor has served at church

Who Gets the Credit for Church Growth?

Pastor Chris cast a vision of what the church could and should be—not a merely good church, but an exceptionally *great* church. Despite the remarkable history of Franklin Downtown Church, Pastor Chris believed that the best years for the church lay ahead. He consistently sought ways to convince lay leaders and members that those best years included them. He helped them clarify their core values as a church: a place where people grow spiritually, love their neighbors and the world, and offer Christ to everyone. For Franklin Downtown Church, growing the church meant growing disciples. Because of the influx of people who had never been affiliated with a church, the congregation began to regularly offer a new member class. In it, newcomers learned what is expected of members: giving a percentage of their income to church ministries, seeking spiritual growth through a small group, and participating in a ministry team that serves others. The change was not without sacrifice. Committed members showed a remarkable willingness to move beyond their own comfort zones. Often giving up personal preferences, they made it possible for the church to offer Christ to the community and a new generation.

Our ideas about pastors tell us more about ourselves than about them. Their office, calling, and authority place pastors in a unique position to make a difference. Nonetheless, pastors and worshipers are cocreators, collaborators, and copilots for the congregation's future. If the dynamics that carry congregations toward growth are like currents in a wide stream, leaders and worshipers must swim in it together. If worshipers' expectations are like tourists'—enjoying the scenery but investing nothing in the life-flowing waters before them—they avoid responsibility for their congregation's ministries. Rather, all who are involved in the congregation must acknowledge and embrace their shared responsibility for the growth of the church.

Questions for Pastors

- What are the congregation's actual core values (not their preferred values) that explain members' motivations and behavior?
- What process is the church using to transform desired values into core values that drive congregational effectiveness?

Questions for Lay Leaders

- Does your congregation spend more time looking back at the past or more time discussing how to press on toward the future?
- What sacrifices are you willing to make as a church to ensure the congregation's future?

OF ALL LEADERSHIP ATTRIBUTES,
THE ONE VALUED MOST AT ST. JUDE'S
WAS RAW PHYSICAL STRENGTH

Chapter 8

What Part Do Pastors Play in Growing Congregational Vitality?

How Are Congregations Strong?

In this chapter, we turn our attention away from numerical growth as a congregational vitality measure. Instead, we look at what makes congregations strong in multiple ways. In our previous research, we detailed ten church health dimensions concentrating on strength. No single congregation possesses all ten strengths. Rather, strong congregations identify three to five areas where they are most effective. A smart, imaginative, and courageous church takes stock of its core mission. After its leaders determine the unique strengths of its ministries, the church then builds on those strengths to leverage even greater ministry effectiveness.

How do congregations show strength? They

1. help their worshipers grow spiritually,
2. provide meaningful worship,
3. are places where worshipers participate in the congregation in many ways,
4. help worshipers find a strong sense of belonging,
5. care for children and youth,
6. focus on the community,
7. encourage worshipers to share their faith with others,
8. welcome new people,
9. rely on empowering congregational leadership, and
10. have a positive outlook on the future.[1]

In our book, *Beyond the Ordinary*, we summarized how these strengths play out in congregations of different sizes, from different faith groups, and with different types of worshipers. Now we answer this important question: What contribution does the pastor make, over and above what worshipers bring, to overall church vitality?

What Gives Us Joy? St Mary's Catholic Parish

St. Mary's religious education program stood out among the parish's many strengths. With Elizabeth's steady leadership, the program attracted talented catechists who built an innovative, effective curriculum. However, when Father John asked Elizabeth one day, "What gives you joy?" he learned that her passion for religious education had shifted. She was increasingly drawn to bereavement ministries because of several recent family deaths. He encouraged her to learn all that she could about these ministries and develop a first-rate ministry for their parish. To relieve Elizabeth of some religious education responsibilities, the parish recruited Martha, a young and enthusiastic newcomer to the community, to serve as the parish's associate director of religious education. Martha and Elizabeth worked together to cultivate stronger parental leadership in the program.

When Father John answered the question, "What gives me joy?" he knew it was the beauty of Catholic worship and liturgy. Father John strongly believed that in worship people encounter God. He presided at Mass in an increasingly thoughtful manner, providing a breath of fresh air to worshipers. With a local architect's help, the worship space was renovated and artfully redesigned. Several decades of neglect had diminished the opportunities for spiritual growth in the parish. Father John began implementing contemporary methods to connect all four adult generations to spiritual growth and formation ministries.

Pastors in Strong Congregations

The ten church strengths individually call for diverse pastoral talents and leadership styles. Therefore, no single pastor profile exists that best fits congregations with each of the ten strengths. Rather, some pastor characteristics are important for predicting one or more congregational strengths. Other pastor profiles predict different strengths. Having analyzed many pastor attributes, we discuss each one in relation to particular strengths (see Figure 8.1). The pastor contributions we present hold true even when we consider many other factors (for example, church size, faith group, and location).[2]

Figure 8.1: Predictors of congregational strengths

Growing spiritually. Where many worshipers are growing in their faith and feel the congregation meets their spiritual needs.

- Married Protestant pastors
- Mainline Protestant male pastors
- First-call pastors
- Conservative Protestant bivocational pastors
- Location—rural areas, small towns or cities
- Faith tradition—Protestant churches
- Small churches

Providing meaningful worship. Where many worshipers experience God's presence, joy, inspiration, and awe in worship services and feel worship helps them with everyday life.

- Pastors who spend less time on administrative tasks
- Location—rural areas, small towns or cities
- Faith tradition—conservative Protestant churches

Participating in the congregation. Where many worshipers attend services weekly and are involved in the congregation in other ways.

- Married Protestant pastors
- Mainline Protestant male pastors
- Conservative Protestant bivocational pastors
- Lifelong pastors
- Pastors who spend more time on preaching and worship leadership, teaching, visiting current members, and pastoral counseling
- Location—rural areas, small towns or cities
- Faith tradition—Protestant churches
- Small churches

Giving a sense of belonging. Where many worshipers have a strong sense of belonging and say most of their closest friends attend the same congregation.

- Married Protestant pastors
- First-call pastors
- Conservative Protestant bivocational pastors
- Second-career pastors
- Faith tradition—Protestant churches

Caring for children and youth. Where many worshipers are satisfied with the offerings for children and youth and have children living at home who also attend there.

- Married Protestant pastors
- Conservative Protestant bivocational pastors
- Pastors serving longer than average in current congregation (more than five years)
- Pastors who spend more time on preaching and worship leadership, teaching, visiting current members, and pastoral counseling
- Location—nonmetropolitan areas
- Faith tradition—Protestant churches
- Larger churches

Focusing on the community. Where many worshipers are involved in social service or advocacy activities and work to make their community a better place to live.

- Seasoned pastors (beyond their first call)
- Full-time pastors
- Pastors who spend more time on administrative tasks
- Location—metropolitan areas
- Faith tradition—mainline Protestant churches, Catholic parishes
- Small churches

Sharing faith. Where many worshipers are involved in evangelism activities and invite friends or relatives to worship.

- First-call pastors
- Mainline Protestant male pastors
- Conservative Protestant bivocational pastors
- Pastors who spend less time on administrative tasks
- Faith tradition—conservative Protestant churches

Welcoming new people. Where many worshipers began attending in the past five years.

- Pastors serving longer than average in current congregation (more than five years)
- Full-time pastors
- Mainline Protestant female pastors
- More reported the congregation experienced some conflict

Empowering leadership. Where many worshipers feel the congregation's leaders inspire others to action and take into account worshipers' ideas.

- Married Protestant pastors
- Pastor serving longer than average in current congregation (more than five years)

- Conservative Protestant pastors who spend more time on preaching and worship leadership, teaching, visiting current members, and pastoral counseling
- Location—metropolitan areas
- Faith tradition—conservative Protestant churches

Looking to the future. Where many worshipers feel committed to the congregation's vision and are excited about the congregation's future.

- Pastors younger than 50
- Married Protestant pastors
- Pastor serving longer than average in current congregation (more than five years)
- Conservative Protestant bivocational pastors
- Faith tradition—conservative Protestant churches

Pastor's age. Pastors of any age can be effective leaders and promote church vitality. Indeed, for nine out of ten strengths, the pastor's age was not relevant. The leader's age predicted only one strength score: looking to the future. Pastors younger than 50 more often lead congregations where many worshipers feel committed to the church's vision and express excitement about its future.

Married Protestant pastors. Married pastors lead almost all Protestant churches: 83% of mainline and 97% of conservative churches. In these churches, a married pastoral leader is the norm, and therefore most worshipers have more familiarity with such leadership. Congregations led by married pastors hold a distinct advantage; these churches' scores tend to be higher for six out of the ten strengths: helping worshipers grow spiritually, participating in the congregation, building a strong sense of belonging, caring for children and youth, empowering congregational leadership, and having a positive outlook on the future. What do these strengths have in common? They converge on the congregation's internal dynamics—how people are involved and what makes them committed participants. That married pastors are more often found in churches with these strengths reflects the traditional nature of most denominations. As more unmarried pastors serve in Protestant churches in coming years, we anticipate that this relationship between congregational strength and the pastors' marital status will change as well.

Gender of mainline Protestant pastors. Women lead mainline Protestant churches that tend to have higher scores on welcoming new people, if all other factors are about the same. However, male mainline Protestant pastors head congregations that are more likely to possess strengths in three other areas: helping worshipers grow spiritually, encouraging worshipers to share their faith, and involving worshipers in congregational activities. As for marital status, we expect the linkages here to weaken as more women move into pastoral positions in the future.

Longer service in current congregation. A pastor with a longer tenure positions the congregation for developing three strengths: caring for children and youth, empowering congregational leadership, and having a positive outlook on the future. Gaining members' trust and the momentum for ministries takes more years in church leadership rather than less. Although longer pastoral tenures seem like a positive for any congregation, this factor is not important for predicting other strengths.

First-call pastors. Pastors serving in their first ministry position bring unique assets–possibly including new ideas and great enthusiasm. Congregations with first-call pastors tend to do well in three areas: helping their worshipers grow spiritually, giving worshipers a strong sense of belonging, and encouraging worshipers to share their faith with others. However, congregations served by first-call pastors tend to lack strength in focusing on the community. Perhaps first-call pastors concentrate on internal priorities and dynamics before they turn to building the congregation's outreach. Developing community relationships that would lead the church into more social service and advocacy work takes additional time.

Bivocational conservative Protestant pastors. Pastors who lead a church and work elsewhere share abundant leadership skills with the church they serve. Bivocational pastors lead one in three conservative Protestant churches. These pastors are rare in Catholic parishes (only 1%) and mainline Protestant churches (only 6%). Conservative Protestant churches that are stronger in helping their worshipers grow spiritually, participating in the congregation, caring for children and youth, and encouraging worshipers to share their faith with others more often have a bivocational pastor. However, tentmakers are not as likely to lead conservative Protestant churches with strength in focusing on the community or welcoming new people. Bivocational pastors may be more likely to concentrate on the congregation's internal affairs, given their more limited time to spend on congregational matters.

Lifelong pastors. Some pastors remain in local church ministry throughout their employment history, serving various congregations over time. These lifelong parish pastors appear to share with their congregations one advantage over pastors who at some point left parish ministry for another setting or secular employment. The strength scores on participating in the congregation were significantly higher in churches served by lifelong pastors.

Pastors' time investments. In a typical week, pastors devote time to many diverse tasks and responsibilities. Pastors estimated the hours per week they spend, including preparation time, in ten task areas.[3] With two exceptions, the proportion of hours invested each week in most tasks was not important for predicting congregational strengths.

First, the proportion of time that pastors spend on administering the work of the congregation, including staff supervision and attending congregational board and committee meetings, typically relates to three strengths. Pastors who spend proportionately *less* time each week on administrative tasks serve in congregations with more strength in providing meaningful worship and encouraging worshipers to share their faith. In contrast, pastors who spend proportionately *more* time each week on administrative tasks typically serve in congregations with more strength in focusing on the community.

Second, the share of hours pastors devote to preaching and worship leadership, teaching people about the faith, pastoral counseling and spiritual direction, and visiting members and their families, including the sick and shut-ins, matters as well. This second set of tasks—all related to ministry with current members—predicts different church strengths. Pastors investing a greater share of their time in ministry tasks with members more often serve in congregations showing strength in participating in the congregation, caring for children and youth, and empowering leadership.

Profile of Strong Congregations

- Small churches develop different strengths than do larger ones.
- Metropolitan churches cultivate different strengths than do those in other locations.
- Diverse pastor profiles are linked to diverse congregational strengths.
- Internally focused strengths emerge in churches led by pastors who devote more time to core ministry tasks.
- Conflict is detrimental to developing congregational strengths.

Congregational Characteristics That Influence Strengths

The pastor's profile does not tell the whole story about what makes congregations strong. Some church features play a part, no matter who leads the congregation.

Church conflict. In most cases, the presence of conflict is not important for predicting congregational strength. In one instance, conflict makes a difference. Congregations that report some level of conflict—minor or major—often demonstrate greater strength in welcoming new people. New people bring new ideas that may generate differences of opinion. Resulting discussions about the congregation's present mission and future vision create opportunities for conflict.

Location. A strong congregation matches its ministry priorities to the people and needs in its location. Churches located in metropolitan areas with populations in excess of 250,000 excel in focusing on the community, which means many worshipers are involved in social service or advocacy efforts. Metropolitan churches also show strength in empowering leadership.

Leaders inspire worshipers to action, and their work makes the community a better place to live.

Churches located in nonmetropolitan places exhibit other strengths. These congregations reveal strength in helping worshipers grow spiritually, providing meaningful worship, involving many worshipers in church activities, and caring for children and youth. This result does not mean that congregations in other locations do not have these strengths. Rather, nonmetropolitan churches are more likely to excel in these ministry areas.

Size of congregation. After taking into account the pastor's profile, church location, and conflict, church size still plays a role in fostering strength. In three ways, small churches have an advantage. They reveal more strength in helping worshipers grow spiritually, participate fully in the congregation's activities, and focus on the local community. Larger churches surpass others in caring for children and youth. Perhaps providing excellent activities for young people requires a critical mass–enough children and youth to offer age-specific programs, for example–and the resources that many worshipers provide to offer quality programs that attract families.

Faith tradition. No other congregational aspect flavors the strength combination as much as the church's faith tradition. The three faith groupings function as a proxy for worshipers' theology and religious beliefs. Faith tradition also reflects an overarching perspective related to local church mission priorities and denominational emphases. In short, while certain tasks are common to all churches, Catholic parishes zero in on some activities and goals, mainline Protestant churches on others, and conservative Protestant churches on yet others.

In general, Protestant churches center their efforts on involving worshipers through many programs and activities beyond worship.[4] As a result, Protestant churches–both mainline and conservative–exhibit strength in helping people grow spiritually, participating in the congregation, building a strong sense of belonging, and caring for children and youth.

Conservative Protestant churches demonstrate more strength in three other ways: providing meaningful worship, encouraging worshipers to share their faith, and engaging worshipers to look to the future.

Finally, when considering the strength of focusing on the community, mainline Protestant churches and Catholic parishes make evident that they see these service and advocacy efforts as high priorities.

Pastor Profile

Empowering Leadership

Lay leaders in a small-town Kansas church carried on its ministry without a pastor for ten years. As members grew older and few new people joined, their concerns about the congregation's future grew. Taking a big risk and all the church's savings, they hired a full-time pastor—a woman fresh out of seminary. She has now served 16 years, and the church's ministries are growing. Their wise investment continues to bear fruit: a second service, creative musical offerings, building renovations, new worshipers, and engaged members using their gifts. This unlikely new pastor believes their choice says, "We have a high trust in spiritual gifts."

What Is the Reward for Pastors?

Pastors experience satisfaction, some job stress, and a sense of accomplishment due to their own efforts and what is happening in the church. Are some congregational strengths associated with better pastoral outcomes?

Our initial hypothesis was that leading a congregation with any of the ten strengths would result in higher pastoral satisfaction and a greater sense of accomplishment. Untangling all the ways congregational strengths might influence pastoral leaders would be impossible. We tested the relationship between each strength and these five pastoral outcomes: ministry satisfaction, life satisfaction, a sense of ministry accomplishment, job stress, and whether ministry impinges on the pastor's private life. Additional dynamics—other than the outcomes we examined—probably play powerful roles as well, but we believe our short list is worth noting.

Positive outcomes. When congregations exhibit strength in six areas—growing spiritually, meaningful worship, sense of belonging, caring for children and youth, empowering leadership, and looking to the future—pastors

---

Figure 8.2: Pastors' experiences associated with congregational strengths

---

Leading a congregation with these strengths yields ministry or personal satisfaction and a greater sense of accomplishment:

- Growing spiritually
- Providing meaningful worship
- Giving a sense of belonging
- Caring for children and youth
- Empowering leadership
- Looking to the future

Leading a congregation with these strengths stresses the pastor, but that is balanced by ministry satisfaction:

- Welcoming new people
- Focusing on the community

Leading a congregation with this strength requires considerable effort, requiring the pastor to counter resistance, conflict, and frustration:

- *Participating in the Congregation*

leading those congregations experience specific positive outcomes (see Figure 8.2). They typically find greater satisfaction in their ministry, a greater sense of accomplishment, and greater life satisfaction. This is not to say that pastors assisting congregations to achieve these high levels of effectiveness do not face challenges such as church conflict, frustration, anxiety, or doubts about ministry. Rather, their leadership experience overall tends to be more positive.

Mixed outcomes. Congregations showing strength in two areas—welcoming new people and focusing on the community—appear to be more taxing for the pastor. In some congregations, worshipers overtly or covertly resist doing things that move their church from an introverted posture (concentrating on what is going on within the church) to an extroverted posture (concentrating on those outside the building). Leading extroverted congregations places greater stress on the pastor, who must deflect tendencies to turn the attention inward. However, leading extroverted congregations benefits the pastor's overall satisfaction with ministry.

Negative outcomes. Congregations showing strength in higher participation levels require more from the pastor. Pastors and members who seek to move their congregation ever forward by increasing involvement in church activities may encounter frustration and conflict. Pastors in such churches experience greater anxiety and stress and related decreased ministry satisfaction.

Pastor for a Few or Pastor for All?

Father John met most members' expectations for a "good" priest. They recognized his strength as a spiritual leader and his generous trust of others' spiritual gifts. Yet not everyone was happy with the new priest. A handful of longtime members missed the special attention they received from the former priest, Father Thomas. He was truly *their* priest—their exclusive chaplain. They resented the new programs, renewed energy, and newcomers. For them, it just wasn't the same parish anymore. Eventually, a few longtime members slipped away to attend a more traditional neighboring parish.

Partners in Building Strength

Positive congregational change requires knowing what to do and how to do it and being motivated to work through conflict resulting from those efforts. In other words, the pastor needs the "how to" and the "want to" (knowledge and motivation). Some pastors feel motivated to obtain and apply this knowledge despite conflict; others do not have that motivation or cannot muster the energy to do so. Likewise, worshipers and lay leadership need openness to change, some level of tolerance for the sacrifices involved, and a willingness to take risks. Together, pastors and worshipers can take positive steps to move the congregation forward.

Questions for Pastors

- What gives you joy? How do you see your passion for ministry connecting with the greatest needs of the congregation and its members?
- How can you and lay leaders build bridges to greater spiritual growth, increased involvement, and deepening friendships?

Questions for Lay Leaders

- In every congregation, something already works well. Can you accurately identify your congregation's strengths?
- How can your congregation build on those strengths? What will work for a congregation of your size, in your location, at this time in your history, with your members, and with the people who live in your community?

CHOICE OF LEADERSHIP STYLE,
AND MATCHING ACCESSORIES,
WERE DAILY CHALLENGES
FOR REV DIMAGGIO

Chapter 9

What Leadership Approaches
Do Pastors Use?

Leadership typologies abound: Ken Blanchard's situational leadership, Paul Stevens and Phil Collins's "equipping pastor," Bill Hybels's ten styles of leadership, Robert Greenleaf's servant leadership, Jim M. Kouzes and Barry Z. Posner's leadership practices, Bernard Bass's transformational leadership, and so on.[1] Understanding common approaches to pastoral leadership enhances our insight into local church ministry. From this broader perspective, we also answer this important question: Does a pastor's leadership influence a congregation's ministry effectiveness?

A Leadership Approach Leads to Conflict:
Pines Community Church

Ed called an emergency meeting of the church board. No one had to ask the reason for the special meeting—their pastor had to go! Ed let everyone express their negative opinions about Pastor Ted before making an announcement. Ed told the board members that he had contacted a denominational official who specialized in helping congregations work through personnel conflicts. The board members reluctantly agreed to work with this outside mediator, although they weren't optimistic that anything would make a difference.

Ted had become increasingly discouraged about his ministry. He listened carefully to every member criticism and every suggestion.

He tried to respond to their requests. Each day seemed longer than the day before as he slogged through his duties. He didn't feel like he was very good at the things the church wanted him to do. Ted's wife noticed he was sleeping more and showing other signs of depression. When he heard that the board had voted unanimously to bring in a denominational official, he felt only relief. One thing was clear: This painful time was going to be over soon, one way or another.

The members of Pines Community Church loved their church and were people of goodwill. They found the conflict surrounding Pastor Ted agonizing. They wanted to make it work. Ted wanted to be a good pastor and the right pastor for the church. But daily, he felt like a square peg being pounded into a round hole. After multiple meetings with the denominational official, Ted realized that he just didn't fit. He submitted his resignation. A few months later, Ted entered a training program for military chaplaincy.

Pastoral Approaches to Leadership

Most leadership theories share the view that leadership is distinct from management. Management involves planning and administering an organization's work on a day-to-day basis. In contrast, leadership entails inspiring and motivating others from a broader perspective to act on the organization's goals. "Management is efficiency in climbing the ladder of success; leadership determines whether the ladder is leaning against the right wall."[2] Pastors take on both managerial and leadership tasks in their ministry work. In this chapter, we spotlight pastoral leadership practices.

Leadership in the congregational context is particularly complex and difficult. First, the leader must negotiate his or her role carefully, because worshipers and members in leadership positions are volunteers. This involves cultivating worshipers' ideas and energies so they remain involved, contributing members. At the same time, the pastor needs to focus worshipers' input and use it to ensure the congregation has a positive future. Second, because worshipers sometimes resist changes, pastors must balance the requirement for new endeavors against the status quo. Third, worshipers who are willing to take on particular tasks or jobs in the church are often inexperienced regarding those tasks. Few church school teachers, for example, bring to that role a professional teacher's education and experience. For the church to succeed, pastors need to encourage rather than alienate their all-volunteer workforce. Finally, pastoral leadership must fit the church context–the specifics of the congregation and the specifics of the community in which it is located.

This chapter explores three facets of leadership: transformational, servant, and inspirational. We identify which types of pastors typically use each approach. Next, we examine how these practices connect to outcomes for congregations and leaders. These three leadership patterns are not mutually exclusive. Pastors often rely on more than one of these overlapping approaches.

Transformational Leadership

Transformational leaders create a sense of loyalty among followers by connecting them to a common organizational vision.[3] People throughout the church feel some ownership in the goals. Transformational pastors also ensure that members look beyond their own interests and toward the church's objectives. Worshipers assist the congregation in moving forward not because they expect personal rewards but rather because they believe in the church's mission.

Transformational pastors offer intriguing and appealing possibilities for the church–ideas that others had not considered. They help worshipers think about problems in new ways. Paying attention to worshipers' needs and helping them learn and grow are hallmarks of transformational pastors. Worshipers trust and have faith in the work that transformational leaders do in their congregation.

Are pastors transformational leaders? We combined eight survey questions to assess the extent to which pastors are transformational leaders.[4] These include enabling others to think of old problems in new ways, helping worshipers find meaning in their involvement, and giving personal attention to those who are less involved. In general, pastors' responses indicate that they believe they are transformational leaders some or most of the time. Catholic, mainline Protestant, and conservative Protestant pastors show similar levels of transformational leadership (see Figure 9.1).

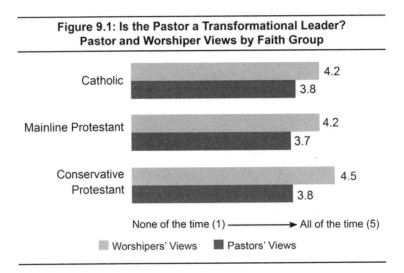

**Figure 9.1: Is the Pastor a Transformational Leader?
Pastor and Worshiper Views by Faith Group**

Catholic
Worshipers' Views: 4.2
Pastors' Views: 3.8

Mainline Protestant
Worshipers' Views: 4.2
Pastors' Views: 3.7

Conservative Protestant
Worshipers' Views: 4.5
Pastors' Views: 3.8

None of the time (1) ⟶ All of the time (5)

▨ Worshipers' Views ■ Pastors' Views

Do worshipers see their pastor as transformational? A random sample of worshipers in each congregation answered the same questions about their pastor's leadership. By combining these items, we created an overall worshiper assessment of the pastor as a transformational leader.[5] In each faith group, worshipers see their leader as more transformational than do the leaders themselves. Does this difference reflect humble leaders who don't want to claim too much in the way of leadership skills? Or does the difference suggest that worshipers perceive transformational ability even though they don't observe their pastor's actions on a day-to-day basis? Perhaps both are true.

Conservative Protestant worshipers see their leader as significantly more transformational than do worshipers in the other two faith groups. Again, we don't know if this mirrors what conservative Protestant worshipers believe effective pastors should be doing or their actual understanding of their leader's approach.

Which pastors are transformational leaders? Several types of pastors are more likely to be transformational leaders:[6]

- **Older, more experienced pastors.** Pastors over age 50, those beyond their first call, and those serving many years in ministry exhibit a more transformational leadership approach than do others.
- **More educated pastors.** Having a master's or doctorate theological degree appears to aid pastors in honing their transformational approach to leadership.
- **Conservative Protestant and Catholic pastors.** When other factors are held constant, we find that conservative Protestant pastors and Catholic priests are more likely than mainline Protestant pastors to be transformational leaders.
- **Women.** In mainline Protestant congregations, female pastors are more likely to be transformational leaders. (There are virtually no female pastors in other types of churches.) Prior research has shown that across many organizations and career fields, women tend to favor collaborative and democratic styles typical of a transformational leader, while men are more directive.[7]

How do transformational leaders experience ministry? A transformational leadership approach yields two positive outcomes. These factors go hand in hand with how such pastors lead:

- **More satisfaction with ministry.** Pastors who embrace the congregation's goals and help others become part of that vision express more satisfaction with their ministry.
- **More enthusiasm for ministry.** Similarly, a wealth of enthusiasm for the work being done drives pastors and supports their transformational way of working with the congregation.

What do transformational leaders bring to their congregation? Pastors who exhibit transformational leadership foster worshipers' positive outlook about the congregation's future—the strength of looking to the future. Although transformational leadership is not directly related to numerical growth, transformational pastors excel in ensuring worshipers see the positive potential for their church's future—an optimistic viewpoint that can spark positive change.

Servant Leadership

Servant leaders make certain that the organization succeeds by focusing on the needs of others: worshipers, other congregational leaders, and those people the church serves. Mother Teresa represents the epitome of servant leadership. Pastors who lead in this manner put serving others first—helping worshipers meet their goals.[8] The primary focus is on the congregation's people—worshipers and staff—in the belief that their motivation to make a difference promotes the church's success. Like transformational leaders, the servant leader involves worshipers in congregational decision making.

Are pastors servant leaders? Our survey included two questions that set servant leadership apart from other approaches. Those questions focus on the pastor's altruism: Does the pastor put the congregation's goals before his or her own interests? Does meeting the worshipers' needs come before meeting the pastor's own needs? Using a measure that combines pastors' answers, our results show that in general pastors view themselves to be altruistic servant leaders.[9] Catholic priests are the most likely to embrace this approach, and mainline Protestant pastors the least likely (see Figure 9.2).

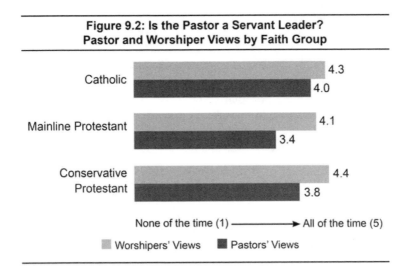

Figure 9.2: Is the Pastor a Servant Leader?
Pastor and Worshiper Views by Faith Group

Catholic
4.3
4.0

Mainline Protestant
4.1
3.4

Conservative Protestant
4.4
3.8

None of the time (1) ⟶ All of the time (5)

☐ Worshipers' Views ■ Pastors' Views

Do worshipers see their pastor as a servant leader? A random sample of worshipers in each congregation answered a similar set of questions about their pastor's servant leadership.[10] Worshipers see their leader more often as a servant leader than do pastors themselves. As we found for transformational leadership, the smallest difference between worshipers' and leaders' views emerged for Catholic priests, and the largest for mainline Protestant pastors. Worshipers in conservative Protestant churches see their pastor as more of a servant leader than do worshipers in other churches.

Which pastors are servant leaders? Only three characteristics of pastors distinguish those who are the most altruistic servant leaders:

- **Conservative Protestant and Catholic pastors.** As Figure 9.2 shows, more conservative Protestant and Catholic pastors than mainline Protestant pastors are servant leaders.
- **Full-time pastors.** Pastors with their entire focus on congregational ministry do not have to split their time and energy between jobs. They excel as servant leaders. Bivocational pastors who serve their congregation while also working in a nonministry job are less likely to be servant leaders.
- **Seven-days-a-week pastors.** Pastors who do not regularly take a day off from ministry, like full-time pastors, devote all their focus to the congregation and are more likely to report being servant leaders.

How do servant leaders experience ministry? Pastors who fit the servant leader profile enjoy several positive outcomes:

- **More enthusiasm for and satisfaction with ministry.** Pastors who put others' needs first are more satisfied with their ministry and express more enthusiasm for their work.
- **Less job stress.** Servant leaders report less job stress than other pastors. Difficulties they might face in ministry are balanced by the satisfaction they experience as they help others achieve their goals.
- **More commitment to staying.** Given the aforementioned positives, it is not surprising that servant leaders thought about leaving their current congregation less often than others.

What do servant leaders bring to their congregation? Pastors who practice selfless servant leadership more often serve in congregations that excel in the strength of sharing faith. Worshipers in congregations with a pastor who favors that approach are better equipped to talk about their faith and invite others to become part of the church.

Inspiring Leadership

Inspiring leaders say that their role is one of motivating and encouraging members to make decisions and take action. Indeed, inspiring leadership overlaps with transformational and servant leadership. We asked pastors to choose one phrase to describe their leadership style.[11] The choices covered inspiring leadership as well as styles in which laity or the pastor makes most decisions (see Figure 9.3).

Are pastors inspirational leaders? Majorities of pastors in each faith group affirm an inspiring, shared leadership approach. Previous research shows that this style is linked to many positive congregational outcomes from giving levels to small-group involvement.[12]

Figure 9.3. How pastors describe their leadership style

	Catholic (%)	Mainline Protestant (%)	Conservative Protestant (%)
Inspiring, shared leadership. I try to inspire and encourage lay members to make decisions and take actions.	70	65	72
Lay-directed congregations. Lay leaders come up with most initiatives or lay leaders make most decisions.	12	33	12
Pastor-directed congregations. I make most of the decisions here.	18	1	17

Some pastors in each faith group rely on other styles. One third of mainline Protestant pastors, yet fewer Catholic and conservative Protestant pastors, report that lay leaders take the initiative to make congregational decisions (lay-directed congregations). Finally, a few pastors make decisions with the expectation that members will follow their lead. Most of these few pastor-directed congregations are Catholic or conservative Protestant churches.

Do worshipers view their pastor as an inspirational leader? We asked worshipers a similar question. Some admitted they couldn't identify the pastor's leadership style. Of those who could, fewer worshipers in each faith group say their pastor is inspirational than do pastors themselves (see Figure 9.4). Perhaps worshipers were drawn to other leadership descriptions that affirmed a larger role for lay leaders in congregational decision making.

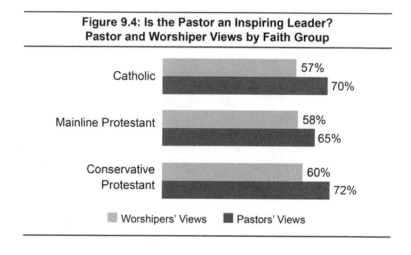

**Figure 9.4: Is the Pastor an Inspiring Leader?
Pastor and Worshiper Views by Faith Group**

Catholic — 57% / 70%

Mainline Protestant — 58% / 65%

Conservative Protestant — 60% / 72%

Worshipers' Views   Pastors' Views

Do pastors and worshipers share a congruent view of leadership?
What are the implications for congregations when worshipers and pastors describe the pastor's leadership style in a similar way? A common view was measured as the percentage of worshipers in the congregation who describe the pastor's leadership style the same way the pastor does (inspirational, lay-directed, or pastor-directed). Across all congregations, a median of 40% of worshipers agree with their pastor's assessment of his or her leadership style. Several positives emerge when pastors and worshipers share a common view:

- **More positive outlook on the future.** When many worshipers and the pastor view the pastor's style the same way, the congregation looks forward to the future and embraces potential change.
- **More faith sharing.** Congregations where the pastor and worshipers hold a consistent view of the leader's style are places where more worshipers comfortably share their faith with others. And more worshipers invite others to visit–the first step in adding new worshipers.
- **Growth.** Numerical growth is more likely when the pastor and worshipers agree on the leadership style used by the pastor.

Putting It All Together

How do these three leadership approaches fit together? Our analyses show that only one in ten pastors can be described as transformational, inspirational, and servant leaders–pastors who draw on *all three* approaches.[13] Rather, most pastors' responses reveal that they lead with a primary approach; some also put a secondary approach in play.

Yet a small number of pastors do not seem to lead in any of the ways we examined. What is going on in these congregations? Most likely they serve as managers in their congregations, rather than leaders. Simply filling the role of pastor in a congregation does not make one a leader because leadership is not determined by role or position. Pastors who *manage* their congregations take care of the day-to-day functioning of the church but do not help worshipers cast a vision for the future. Such congregations drift without direction and may stagnate. Without leadership a congregation will not move forward. In fact, these managerial pastors who do not lead in any of the ways covered here are less likely than other pastors to report their congregation is always ready to try new things. Fewer managerial pastors say that worshipers have a sense of excitement about the congregation's future. The implications are clear: leadership, not management, is what makes a difference.

Overall, worshipers see their pastors as more transformational and servant-like than pastors see themselves. On the other hand, more pastors think they are inspirational leaders than their worshipers do. In part, these pastor-worshiper discrepancies result from different experiences. Only worshipers who are highly involved in their congregation gain day-to-day contact with their pastor. Other worshipers have limited insight into the pastor's leadership practices outside of worship. Seeing a pastor leading worship services probably highlights a transformational image because preaching often encourages people to see things in new ways and fosters learning. Both of these are elements of transformational leadership.

Profile of Pastoral Leadership Approaches

- Pastors use a variety of leadership approaches or strategies.
- Worshipers see their pastors as servant and transformational leaders.
- Pastors see themselves as servant leaders, transformational leaders, and inspiring leaders.
- Conflict is more common in lay-directed congregations.

Leadership and Conflict

Now we turn to the relationship between leadership and congregational conflict. Three quarters of pastors report that their congregation experienced conflict recently. What did they report the conflict was about? Some aspect of pastoral leadership style was most common (see Chapter 3). Given pastors' perceptions that conflict is linked to their leadership, examining this linkage is worthwhile. Are any of the three leadership approaches we've examined related to the presence or absence of congregational conflict?

The three leadership approaches are more common in congregations that are *free from conflict.* Fewer transformational pastors and servant leader pastors report serving churches that dealt with minor or major conflict in recent times. Similarly, those pastors who describe their leadership as inspiring worshipers to action typically serve where conflict is not a problem.

True leadership minimizes conflict because it creates a shared vision and common direction for the congregation. When all worshipers embrace the vision, they trust the pastor to help them achieve their goals.

Conflict is reported most often in congregations where *laity* take the initiative in making decisions and planning congregational programs (lay-directed congregations, as shown in Figure 9.3). Three in ten lay-directed congregations (30%) experienced major conflict in recent years. Only two in ten churches where the leadership is inspirational and shared with laity (21%) encountered conflict. Lay-directed churches may lack effective leaders. In a leadership vacuum, different worshipers might attempt to take the church in different directions, resulting in conflict that the pastor cannot handle.

What Kind of Leadership Works for Our Church?

The members at Pines Community Church did not realize that they did not know much about leadership. In reality, different factions held different views on leadership. Some members wanted a transformational leader—a pastor who would bring exciting ideas and a common vision to the congregation. Another group wanted an inspiring leader—a pastor who would encourage lay leaders' gifts and share the leadership role with them. A third group in the congregation felt they could do just fine without a pastor. This group shared a tribe mentality—the pastor is not one of us, and we simply have to tolerate him. Pastor Ted, the compromise candidate, satisfied none of these groups. His leadership approach came closest to a servant leader model—for example, he excelled in one-on-one pastoral care. He managed the church assuming that if he took care of members' emotional and spiritual needs, then lay leaders would take the initiative on organizational matters and big-picture decision making. The resulting leadership vacuum allowed various individuals to take the church in opposite directions. In the end, blind spots on both sides led to inevitable church conflict.

Pastor Profile

Purveyors of Hope

Congregations look for pastors with emotional maturity and intelligence. Churches need pastors who are prepared for ministry and show resiliency. Members want enthusiastic pastors who know the difference between being managers and leaders. Most of all, pastors should be purveyors of hope.

Marcia Clark Myers, director of the Office of Vocation, Presbyterian Church (USA), February 5, 2008.

Building More Effective Leaders

This chapter illustrates that many pastors use specific leadership approaches to successfully lead congregations. Yet leadership is not a static, you-are-or-you-aren't skill. It's not a trait that people are born with. In fact, leadership has been called "an ongoing process of growing, evolving, and developing."[14] How can pastors and other congregational leaders become excellent leaders? Leadership can be learned, and regular practice strengthens leadership skills. Research has found that learning leaders are effective leaders. They do the following:

- Spend more time in learning activities. Literally, they engage in learning by reading, talking with others, experimenting with new ways of doing things or reflecting on their own leadership behaviors.
- Ask more questions.
- Don't assume they know everything.
- Aren't afraid to admit mistakes.
- Ask for feedback, and when they get it they say "thank you" and accept it as a gift by taking it seriously, whether the feedback is positive or negative.
- Encourage others to experiment, take risks and accept failure by asking "What can we learn?"[15]

Effective leadership begins with a conscious choice to *become* a leader. From there, the path forward involves developing leadership abilities through reading, education, and–foremost–practice. Pastors who are committed to improving their leadership represent the best future for congregations. Seminaries, denominations, judicatories, parachurch organizations, and others can assist pastors by offering practical educational and developmental options that address church leadership. Congregations, too, can lend support by giving their pastor the time needed to pursue such learning. Worshipers can accompany their pastor on this journey, accepting his or her leadership efforts that might not work out as hoped; offering gentle, helpful feedback; and encouraging continued practice. Leading congregations into the future is the "secret ingredient" that moves simply adequate churches toward becoming excellent places of worship.

Questions for Pastors

- What is the best description of your leadership approach? Ask three to five people who know you well to describe your pastoral leadership approach. Does their description match yours?

- In conversations with lay leaders, what do you learn about their assumptions regarding effective pastoral leadership? How can this information inform your leadership?

Questions for Lay Leaders

- Thinking about your current and previous pastors, did the leadership approach of one pastor seem to fit your church best? Why do you think that approach was most effective?
- What steps can your congregation take to help your pastor become a more effective leader?

Chapter 10

What Makes for the Best Pastor-Congregation Match?

What contributes to perceptions by a pastor and the church's worshipers that there is a good match between them? Here we seek to identify the church features that produce worshipers' satisfaction with their pastor. Likewise, specific factors ensure that pastors believe their leadership fits the congregation well. What are these conditions? Does a positive match perception result in higher pastoral satisfaction in ministry, for example? Does this beneficial perception impact church vitality? In this chapter, we investigate both the predictors of a "good match" verdict and the outcomes of agreement between pastor and congregation.

Is There a Good Leadership Match?

Half of worshipers *strongly* agree with the statement "In general, there is a good match between our congregation and our minister, pastor, or priest."[1] Another third simply agree with the statement. A very small number of worshipers (only 3%) believe their pastor and congregation are not a good match, and the rest are neutral or unsure (12%). These findings suggest a high level of worshiper satisfaction with their current leader.

How do pastors feel about the fit between their leadership and the congregation? We asked pastors if they agree with a similar statement: "In general, there is a good match between this congregation and my leadership." Overall, 45% of pastors *strongly* agree. This means slightly fewer pastors than worshipers strongly agree that there is a good pastoral leadership match (50% of worshipers strongly agree; 45% of pastors strongly agree).

Typically, worshipers and leaders do not understand the leadership match in exactly the same way. In many cases, worshipers see the match between the congregation and the pastor's leadership more positively than the leader perceives the match. Figure 10.1 reveals how far apart worshiper and leader perceptions about the match tend to be. Catholic priests rate the leadership match lower than parish worshipers (49% of worshipers strongly agree; only 29% of Catholic priests strongly agree). Of the three faith traditions, the gap between worshiper and pastor perceptions about the leadership match is largest among Catholics.

In contrast, mainline Protestant pastors tend to consider the match between their leadership and the congregation more positively than do their worshipers (45% of worshipers strongly agree, but 53% of pastors strongly agree). As in Catholic parishes, conservative Protestant pastors rate the match less positively than do their worshipers (60% of worshipers strongly agree; only 42% of their pastors strongly agree).

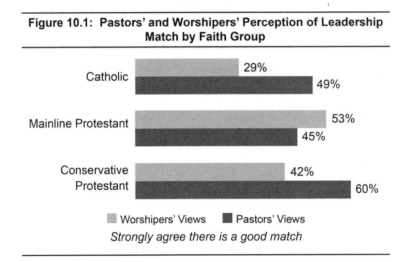

Figure 10.1: Pastors' and Worshipers' Perception of Leadership Match by Faith Group

Measuring the good match. To combine worshiper and pastor perceptions into a single match indicator, we first identified congregations where the pastor feels his or her leadership is a good match (either strongly agree or agree; 78%). Next, we calculated the percentage of worshipers in those congregations who strongly agree with the match statement "In general, there is a good match between our congregation and our minister, pastor, or priest." Thus both the pastor and a percentage of worshipers *agree* there is a good pastor-congregation match. On average, less than half of worshipers (44%) agree with their leader that a good match exists in their congregation. A very small number of congregations score zero on this pastor-congregation agreement measure because the pastor does not believe it is a good leadership match (13%). The rest of this chapter's discussion focuses on the predictors and outcomes of the combined perceptions of pastors and worshipers—*the pastor-congregation match agreement.*

While the pastor-congregation agreement about the leadership match varies from one congregation to another, faith tradition plays a part (see Figure 10.2). In general, conservative Protestant churches have the highest level of

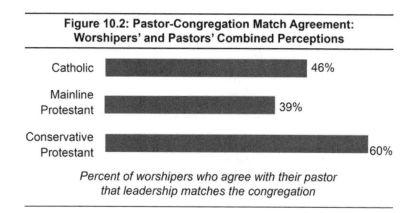

Figure 10.2: Pastor-Congregation Match Agreement: Worshipers' and Pastors' Combined Perceptions

Catholic 46%

Mainline Protestant 39%

Conservative Protestant 60%

Percent of worshipers who agree with their pastor that leadership matches the congregation

pastor-congregation match agreement (median score is 60%). Catholic parishes typically fall below that high mark (46%). Mainline Protestant churches report the lowest level of pastor-congregation match agreement (39%).

What Predicts the Combined Perception of a Good Pastor-Congregation Match?

The following questions call attention to the predictors and outcomes of the combined perceptions of pastors and worshipers—*the pastor-congregation match agreement.* First, we summarize the part pastors play in perceptions about a good leadership match. Then we review the congregational characteristics that relate to a good leadership match.

What pastor characteristics are associated with greater pastor-congregation match agreement? We considered demographics (such as age, marital status, second career), pastors' activities (such as time spent on ministry tasks), and their leadership styles. Only a few pastoral qualities are associated with higher pastor-congregation match agreement scores:[2]

- **The pastor has served the congregation longer than average.** The combined perception of a good pastor-congregation match increases with the number of years the pastor has served there. Longer tenure affords the chance to build stronger relationships and a more fruitful ministry. Conversely, when both the pastor and worshipers believe the match is not a good one, the pastor is more likely to have already found another call. Likewise, unhappy worshipers sometimes leave when they feel the pastor is not the best leader for the congregation. Thus those worshipers remaining in the congregation are more likely to report that they see the pastor's leadership as a good match for the church.

- **The pastor devotes less time than average to teaching.** Like the rest of us, pastors only have so many hours in a day. The choices they make about how to invest their time reveal something about their priorities. When pastors report spending a greater share of work hours on teaching people about the faith, the pastor-congregation match agreement drops. In this situation, worshipers fail to see the leadership as a good match for the congregation. However, when the pastor makes other ministry tasks–such as preaching and visitation–a priority, there is more agreement between pastor and worshipers about the leadership match.

What aspects of the congregation are associated with a better pastor-congregation agreement? Multiple congregational dynamics relate to a good pastor-congregation match agreement:

- **Less conflict.** In congregations with less conflict, more pastors and worshipers agree that the leadership match is good.
- **Less pastoral turnover.** A smaller number of pastors serving a congregation over the past ten years is associated with a better sense of a pastor-congregation match. Granted, having fewer pastors over a ten-year period is also correlated with the length of the pastor's tenure (see previous section on pastor characteristics). But even taking that and other factors into account, high leadership turnover is detrimental to the current pastor-congregation match assessment.

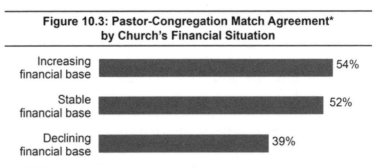

Figure 10.3: Pastor-Congregation Match Agreement*
by Church's Financial Situation

Increasing financial base	54%
Stable financial base	52%
Declining financial base	39%

*NOTE: Percentages shown are worshipers who strongly agree their pastor is a good match for the congregation in churches where the pastor also agrees that his or her leadership is a good match.

- **Favorable church finances.** When congregations describe their financial base as increasing or stable, their pastor-congregation match agreement is higher. Conversely, congregations where the financial situation is declining or a serious threat to their viability assess the fit as less positive (see Figure 10.3).

Are congregational strengths associated with a good pastor-congregation match agreement? We found some of the ten congregational strengths are related to more agreement between pastors and worshipers regarding the congregational match. A few church strengths appear to be more central to pastors' and worshipers' sense that the pastor's leadership is right for the congregation:

- **Providing meaningful worship.** In congregations where many worshipers experience God's presence, joy, inspiration, and awe in worship services and feel worship helps them with everyday life, pastors and worshipers agree the leadership match is good.
- **Giving a sense of belonging.** In churches where many worshipers have a strong sense of belonging and say most of their closest friends attend the same congregation, the pastor and many worshipers rate the match as good.
- **Caring for children and youth.** In churches where many worshipers are satisfied with the offerings for children and youth and have children living at home who also attend there, the pastor and more worshipers rate the match as good.
- **Empowering leadership.** In congregations where many worshipers feel the congregation's leaders inspire others to action and take into account worshipers' ideas, the pastor and many worshipers rate the match as good.[3]
- **Looking to the future.** In congregations where many worshipers feel committed to the congregation's vision and are excited about the congregation's future, the pastor and more worshipers agree the leadership fits the church.

What Are the Pastoral Outcomes of a Good Pastor-Congregation Match?

A congregation thrives when the pastor and worshipers take the church's temperature and get the same reading. The road to effective ministry is paved when pastor and worshiper opinions about how things are going coincide. Pastors climbing rocky paths of resistance may suffer from disappointment, frustration, and stress. Is there evidence that pastors' ministry satisfaction or lower job-related stress signals a better pastor-congregation match agreement? Yes. Several positive pastoral outcomes forge a good pastor-congregation assessment:

- **Greater enthusiasm for ministry.** When worshipers and pastors reach high levels of agreement about the leadership match, pastors are more enthusiastic about their work.
- **Greater personal satisfaction.** Positive feelings about the leadership match by both the pastor and worshipers affirm all who are involved. The upbeat nature of the current ministry setting spills over into pastors' satisfaction with private life, too.
- **Better emotional health.** We found that pastors serving in congregations with higher pastor-congregation agreement scores enjoy better emotional health as well. Certainly, serving as a pastor where many worshipers believe the match is poor would be damaging and difficult for anyone.
- **Less job stress.** Pastors experience less stress when they and the congregation's worshipers believe the leadership match is good. Discontent in the pew breeds greater stress for pastors.
- **Pastors choose to remain in the congregation.** Finally, one of the most important outcomes of a good pastor-congregation match agreement is stability—the pastor is more likely to stay put. When the pastor and/or worshipers do not believe the pastor's leadership is the right one for the church, pastors consider seeking another place to serve. When many worshipers consider the match a poor one, pastors are far more likely to leave for another congregation.

Pastor Profile

Butchers, Potters, and Pastors—Shaping the Material at Hand

My father was a butcher. His meat market was within walking distance of our home. Not so much by words but by example, I internalized a respect for the material at hand. The material could be a pork loin, or a mahogany plank, or a lump of clay, or the will of God, or a soul, but when the work is done well, there is a kind of submission of will to the conditions at hand, a cultivation of what I would later learn to call humility. It is a noticeable feature in all skilled workers—woodworkers, potters, poets, pray-ers and pastors. I learned it in the butcher shop.

Eugene H. Peterson, excerpt from *The Pastor: A Memoir,* as it appeared in *Christian Century*, February 22, 2011, 28–29.

The Necessity of a Good Pastor-Congregation Match

Reaching a good leadership fit comes with high stakes. When the leadership match does not work, the pastor is much more likely to leave and the church suffers. Congregations with empty pulpits circle and wait for new leadership to arrive. The congregation incurs the financial costs of calling a new pastor, may experience membership decline, and often attracts few new members during this holding pattern.

A recent study of why pastors leave local church ministry found that a minority (30–40%) left involuntarily. The majority of pastors who left voluntarily reported both pull factors drawing them elsewhere (such as the offer of a new ministry position) and push factors urging them away from their current church (such as conflict or frustration over lack of progress). Too often when church conflict occurs, members assume the pastor must be at fault. However, the researchers concluded that the majority of pastors left for organizational reasons, not personal ones (such as illness or misconduct).[4]

Profile of a Good Pastor-Congregation Match

- Pastors and worshipers understand a good match differently.
- Conflict and pastoral turnover are detrimental to a good match.
- Stable or increasing church finances are linked to a good match.
- The congregational strengths of meaningful worship, caring for children and youth, empowering leadership, and looking to the future are connected to a good match.
- A good match yields ministry satisfaction, less stress, and commitment to the congregation for the pastor.

How Can Congregations Achieve a Good Pastor-Congregation Match?

What insights can we gain from the experiences of Chris at Franklin Downtown Church, Ted at Pines Community Church, and John at St. Mary's Catholic Parish?

- A pastor's perceptions about the effectiveness of his or her leadership rarely match worshipers' perceptions.
- A careful process to prepare for a new pastor can set the stage for more realistic expectations by the pastor and congregation. Lay leaders should address any unresolved church conflict before the new pastor arrives.
- When churches take stock of their current strengths and challenges, they gain greater insight into the kind of pastor who could best lead them into the future. Their blueprint for what is to come answers three questions: Who are we? (our core values and history); who is our neighbor? (our mission and ministry outreach); and why are we here? (our primary calling in this geographic location).
- Pastors help lay leaders understand the congregation's situation when they communicate how larger societal and cultural trends are likely to impact the church's ministries.

- Some church members say, "We want our church to grow!" but staunchly resist any change that could make that happen. Their opposition shows that their actual core values are inconsistent with their stated goals.
- The congregation's financial sustainability plays an important part in determining the most workable staffing model. For example, can the church afford salary and benefits for a full-time pastor for the next three to five years? If not, what other staffing arrangement might work?
- All churches need a group that deals with personnel issues—a personnel, staff-parish relations, or pastoral relations committee. This group holds responsibility for offering encouragement, advice, and counsel to the pastor. Working with the pastor, their mission is to help the pastor, other staff, lay leaders, and members do a better job in their ministries.[5]
- Pastors and lay leaders operate with blind spots, unspoken assumptions, and invisible agendas. Ongoing communication helps all parties surface unquestioned ideas about the best approaches to ministry.
- Despite sincere efforts, it takes one to two years for the pastor and church to get to know each other well. Then it takes a year or so for them to get over it.[6]
- Big changes take time. Pastors can get ahead of the congregation by proposing too many changes too quickly.
- Conflict happens. We have our differences of opinion. Pastors with conflict management skills prevent minor disagreements from escalating into major wars.
- Pastors flourish when they are able to pursue the aspects of ministry they are most passionate about and spend time in ministry areas that give them the greatest satisfaction. This is almost never church administration.
- All pastors benefit from opportunities for personal and professional development.
- Some pastoral traits are irrelevant to predicting a good congregation-pastor match. Others turn out to be highly important. If the pastor's vision for ministry, ministry strengths, and commitment to spiritual growth fit the congregation's assets and needs, the chances for a good match improve dramatically.

When the pastor and congregational leaders explicitly state and agree on reasonable expectations, the groundwork for a good match is laid. Working toward common goals unites everyone in the congregation. When mission priorities are lost in translation, neither party arrives at effective ministry.

Questions for Pastors

- What factors go into your assessment about whether your leadership is a good match for the congregation? Are your perceptions flavored by the loudly expressed views of a few members?
- Does the congregation have a group that deals with personnel issues, such as a staff-parish relations or pastoral relations committee? Do you meet regularly with this group to receive feedback and constructive evaluations? How do you use that information?

Questions for Lay Leaders

- As you think about the church's needs and your pastor's leadership gifts, do you see a good match? From your perspective, what are the key pieces for understanding the puzzle of an excellent match?
- During your current pastor's tenure, how much have the church's needs changed?
- How have your perceptions of the pastor's effectiveness changed? What's behind that change?

Chapter 11

Implications

Franklin Downtown Church, Pines Community Church, and St. Mary's Catholic Parish all navigated the ups and downs of pastoral transition. What did they take away from the process? Is there anything we can learn from what happened in these churches?

What Didn't Work Before Still Doesn't Work: Franklin Downtown Church

Three years after beginning at Franklin Downtown Church, Chris ran into a seminary classmate at a national conference. His classmate was in the process of seeking a new church call and wanted to know if Chris had any advice. "Sure!" Chris replied, "You might as well avoid some of the walls I walked into!" Chris set the stage by noting that the previous pastor, who had served for 17 years, talked about his upcoming retirement for five years. Chris didn't know if it was an intentional strategy–but it worked. Members were so tired of hearing about it that they actually began to look forward to his departure! Chris shared that he favors the interim pastor model in most cases. Franklin Downtown Church's identity had become so merged with this long-serving previous pastor that as he lost interest, the church's energy declined as well.

An interim pastor worked for more than two years to get the congregation ready to call Chris. Chris said he admired the fact that lay leaders trusted the process, even though it took extra time and effort. He related that sometimes weeks went by before he heard back from the pastor search committee. That confused him–did it mean they weren't interested in calling him, or did it signal some kind of organizational dysfunction? He wished the committee had been better about timely communication. However, he was impressed with their honesty and self-awareness. Chris explained how clear the lay leaders were about the ways they wanted the church to change. They also made explicit what they expected to stay the same: a theologically moderate church with traditional worship and a strong Christian education program.

Chris's classmate expressed amazement at how much he knew about the church before becoming their pastor. Chris reported that the search committee did something that was extremely helpful: They provided "church references"–three people (and their contact information) who were well informed about the church. One reference was a church member; another, a regional denominational official; and the third, a local community leader. Through phone conversations, Chris learned valuable information about the church and community:

> Even though Franklin Downtown Church members said they wanted change, they were reluctant to downsize their wieldy committee structure. I think some people thought that with a new pastor, everything would work better. After a while, they realized that even with a new pastor, their committee structure still wasn't working. Instead of trying to convince them that was true, I figured it was better to wait and let them discover that on their own.
>
> If I had to do it over again, I'd seek out more peer support right from the beginning. I needed a lot of help in the first year or two with sermon preparation, church administration, and conflict management. Because I'd been an associate pastor, I thought I knew more than I did. I wear a lot of different hats every single day, so I have to manage my time more carefully. If I take on too much, there isn't extra staff to help out.

Chris's classmate wanted to know what the members were like. Chris replied,

> They're great! The church has many talented lay leaders who are patient and supportive. I'll never forget my first Sunday preaching. I was so nervous. A church elder slipped me a note minutes before the service began. It read 'We came to worship God today. We have not come to criticize you, but to pray with and for you. May God bless you and the ministry of our church.' That note sums up the kind of support they've given me since Day 1.

Damaged from the Start: Pines Community Church

After Ted's resignation, the denominational official who helped Pines Community Church work through their conflict returned. He met with the church board and pastor search committee, hoping to encourage them to use a different approach to call their next pastor. Ed was the first to speak: "We really laid down the tracks for this train wreck long before Pastor Ted visited the church. We had not done the hard work of figuring out our church's fundamental mission." Other heads nodded in response. Ed was brave in naming one of their challenges: the many different ideas about what the church's priorities should be. By calling Pastor Ted, a compromise candidate, they satisfied no one. Susan admitted that they didn't fully appreciate that not all pastors are the same.

The lessons for lay leaders. The denominational official suggested they outline the steps that they would take to call their new pastor. Hoping for a better pastor-congregation match next time, they listed these actions:

- Develop a process and timeline and share it widely with members. Give frequent updates about their progress.
- Conduct in-home listening sessions with members, and use the findings to summarize the congregation's mission priorities, current strengths, and financial picture.
- Form a new pastor search committee that has representatives from all groups in the church: young adults, new members, long-term members, parents, choir members, and others.
- Consider pastors whose ministry strengths align with the church's priorities and values.
- Invite at least three pastors to talk with the pastoral search committee. Ask all pastors the same set of questions (written by the committee in advance). Be candid and ask even uncomfortable questions that are essential for determining if the pastor matches the church's priorities.
- Contact references or others who know each pastor the committee is seriously considering. Ask them to confirm the pastor's ministry gifts and leadership approach.
- Learn strategies to deal with conflict among committee members.

The lessons for Pastor Ted. Another chaplain in Ted's training program asked him about his experiences as a local church pastor. Ted's new colleague was curious about why someone with Ted's obvious abilities would make such an abrupt career change. Ted admitted that his last church was not a great place for him or his family. "I know people don't talk about everything before they go to a new church, but I really neglected to ask important questions." Ted went on to say that his lack of knowledge about the situation wasn't all that created problems. He accepted that he hadn't really understood what he enjoyed about ministry and what he was good at. Ted likes dealing with people one-on-one and wasn't interested in the management challenges in a local church. He also wished he had known more about the church's finances before arriving. Ted told his colleague that he believes church financial sustainability means something different now than it did in the past. He felt unable to communicate effectively about the larger cultural issues that affected the church's future. In fact, he believes that the ministry model preferred by the majority of the church's members no longer fits their community context.

An Appointed Pastor: St. Mary's Catholic Parish

Father John met with a soon-to-be-reappointed associate pastor. The Archbishop wanted Father John to offer encouragement and support to his colleague as he made the transition to being a pastor. The two priests, Father John and Father Xavier, met for coffee. Xavier pulled out his notes–he had a lot of questions for Father John! John laughed when he saw the long list. "I know exactly how you feel. It is both terrifying and exhilarating to think about all that responsibility."

Father Xavier asked, "Well, what's the first thing you would do?" Father John suggested that he check out his new parish by driving around and asking people in the grocery store or other shops what they know about the parish. He also recommended that Xavier talk with the outgoing pastor and seek the following information:

- If you were making a list of this parish's greatest strengths, what would you put at the top of that list?
- If you were making a list of things in which this parish is not as strong as you wish it were, what would be the first one or two items on that list?
- If you were making a list of the parish's most cherished values, what would be the first one or two items on that list?
- When people talk about the best priest this parish ever had, what did he do best?
- When people talk about priests in the past who were not very effective, what did they do poorly?
- When this parish considers a major decision, in your experience, is there a group or a couple of individuals that usually exert a strong influence in any discussion?

Father Xavier moved on to his next question: "Do you think there is a right priest for every parish?" Father John hesitated before finally speaking. "Yes, for most churches, but not 100% of them." He gave examples of two circumstances in which no pastor could be effective. He explained that in some churches the people only "tolerate" the priest because they have their own way of doing things. Pastors come and go, but many long-term members provide all the continuity. The church operates as a family chapel, and that makes it hard for any priest to be accepted as a member of the family. The second situation involves a parish served by a superstar pastor. John knew a fellow priest who was appointed to follow this kind of dynamic leader. It didn't matter what the new pastor did–never was he compared favorably to the former pastor. John remarked that he felt this was one of the negatives for denominations that appoint pastors. Typically, there is no interim pastor and no transition period for worshipers to take stock of their church's needs. In effect, some pastors become the unintentional interim.

Finally, Father John laid out another piece of wisdom:

> You know, it isn't always clear that seeking a good match between the pastor and the parish is the highest priority for Church officials when appointments are made. Ignoring the need for a good fit conveys the message that pastors are all alike and just interchangeable parts in a larger system.

Father John told Father Xavier that he had several older cousins who also became priests:

> Because I grew up with those guys, I know pastors are just ordinary people. But my cousins are men who one day recognized that God was calling them for a special ministry. I think this knowledge has always helped me keep a grounded perspective. However, because we are called by God, we bear the greatest responsibility in being the best pastor for our parish.

Research Highlights: Strong Pastor + Strong Lay Leadership

We challenge the illusion that if a congregation has the right leader, everything goes well, and without the right leader, everything goes wrong. With this erroneous view, the secret to congregational vitality revolves around finding the right leader at the right time. Much of the writing about vital congregations places enormous stock in the deception that lay leadership is inconsequential. One religious researcher argues that increasing individualism and congregationalism has fostered the false pastor-led, passive-laity vision. The writer concludes, "Even a strong pastorate is not enough if it is not coupled with a strong lay leadership."[1] Finding the best pastor-laity leadership fit for a specific church is an essential art. Based on the research findings presented here, we believe several implications are worth highlighting.

Learning from the past. God does not call pastors to replicate the past.[2] Yet knowing what pastor characteristics and leadership approaches helped the congregation in the past is crucial. No other reflection gives church leaders better insight into a good pastor-congregation match. Lay leadership benefits from reflecting on the ministry of previous pastors by sharing answers to these questions:

* What did your last two pastors do extremely well? How were they most effective?
* What gaps did you observe in their ministries?
* What activities or programs did they start that you would not like to give up?
* What changes did they make that you would like to continue?

- What activities or programs did they start that most of the members would be willing to let go?

Surface unstated assumptions. Lay leadership and worshipers must first be honest with themselves before they can be honest with their pastor. Worshipers sometimes hold unstated preferences regarding the pastor's profile—such as his or her age, gender, marital status, number of children, seminary education, years in ministry, and career history. As we have documented, new categories of people are being called to ministry. If congregational leaders are not aware of these changes, churches might call or expect the same sort of pastor they have had in the past. Lay leadership and denominational leaders should consider casting a broader net than ever before.

One useful exercise involves asking those responsible for screening ministry candidates to write an "ideal candidate" profile, listing as many characteristics as possible. Review each entry together, honestly discussing what assumptions support each preference. Remove any items the group realizes are not related to effective ministry. Interview and consider only the candidates that match the items on the list. Calling or placing a pastor that does not match the desired profile sets up the pastor and church for frustration and failure.

Financial responsibility matters. As more congregations struggle with financial issues, clergy compensation decisions become more problematic. Both the pastor and church must be honest: the pastor about personal and family financial obligations, and the congregation about their expectations. If worshipers ask their pastor to lead but make little time or financial investment in the church themselves, the pastor is treated more or less as a hired hand. As a result, shared leadership is truly nonexistent. The pastor should be clear about family needs and his or her willingness (and ability) to devote significant hours each week to church ministry. When the pastor and congregational leadership share readily understood expectations, churches reduce miscommunication and conflict.

Conflict damages congregations and pastors. Minor conflict is normative in church life. Yet ongoing disputes and major conflict, which may result in pastors or worshipers leaving, erode congregational vitality. Pastors serving in congregations free of conflict find greater satisfaction in ministry, experience less stress, and maintain clearer boundaries between ministry and their personal life.

Pastors depart from churches when they are unsuccessful at balancing ministry satisfaction and job stress. When worshipers see the pastor leading—using a transformational, servant, or inspiring approach—conflict less often becomes an issue. Finally, when pastors and worshipers agree about the best leadership approach for the congregation, minor conflict remains minor.

Ongoing clergy support is needed. Pastors need ongoing support from the congregation, their peers, their denomination, and seminaries.

Congregations that adequately support clergy receive far more in return. Pastors thrive when they take time for family, personal interests or hobbies, exercise, rest or renewal, study, and spiritual practices. Reasonable expectations from lay leadership assist pastors in time management and appropriate self-care. How pastors spend their time reflects their priorities. If good communication and a common vision exist, the pastor's time investments will mirror the congregation's priorities as well.

Identify and build on strengths. Dr. Groopman, an oncologist, and Dr. Hartzband, an endocrinologist, strive to help doctors and patients communicate more intelligently. As optimists, they warn against the "focusing illusion—focusing on what will be lost after a colostomy, mastectomy, prostate surgery, or other major procedures." They write that the "focusing illusion neglects our extraordinary capacity to adapt, to enjoy life with less than 'perfect' health."[3] Congregations fall prey to a focusing illusion when they identify with past success or dwell on what must be given up if the church is to flourish in the future. Other harmful illusions include the belief that the church can be good at everything or that a perfect pastor can solve all problems.

Congregations possess extraordinary capacity and strength. Grasping what makes congregations strong is more helpful than emphasizing organizational weaknesses. Congregations hold a dual essence—part universal and part unique. All congregations exist as houses of worship. Churches also create spaces for emotional bonding, educate people about their faith and religious practices, assist worshipers in sharing that faith with others, serve people in need, convey messages of hope, and point to ultimate meaning. The unique avenues by which congregations direct these universals reveal their unique strengths. Across ten distinct congregational strengths, we found that no single congregation displays all ten. Rather, a single congregation typically emphasizes three to five areas where it excels in ministry. We encourage church leaders to name these strengths, understand how they were developed, and then leverage existing strengths to build additional ministry effectiveness.[4]

What is God calling our church to be in this place? Most pastors come from larger churches and are trained to serve in such settings. Yet the majority of congregations are small and located in nonmetropolitan areas. Can pastors and lay leadership develop realistic expectations about pastoral ministry that match the real world of the local church?

All places belong to God. Only for a time are places entrusted to us. In the most fundamental sense, a congregation's location is its birthright. Congregations develop place scripts—a way of thinking about their location. These scripts are necessary for a congregation's identity. They identify the congregation's goals, help cement a sense of purpose, and supply a feeling of security. However, the congregation's location script can either fit or be at odds with its present core values. The script can shape the congregation's perception of its place in a positive and energizing way. Or the script can be negative and limiting. Sometimes the scripts of place are well articulated, but often they are implicit, even unconscious. Articulating the congregation's script means learning from church history, checking for consistency in worshiper and pastoral understanding of God's purposes, and imagining a new ministry chapter.[5]

What can we expect? Early settlers built dams on Maine's rivers to harness the water's power. Their mills and factories ran by this nature-generated force. Later the dams produced electricity for business and industry. Today, Maine has more than a thousand dams on its 31,000 miles of rivers, even though many no longer serve their original purpose. Only 111 of Maine's dams still produce electricity. Because the dams altered the rivers' natural functioning, a broad coalition of groups has worked carefully for decades to remove them for safety, environmental, and economic reasons. The return of Atlantic salmon, alewives, sea-run brook trout, and other fish prove that these efforts make a difference.

The exact number of dams in Maine is unknown. Thus one obstacle to future dam removal is simply finding them. Dams four feet or greater in height have been mapped. However, hundreds of smaller dams have never been located and recorded. The only way to discover these petite dams is to kayak down the river.[6]

In an earlier chapter, we described the dynamics that carry congregations forward as similar to currents in a wide river. We mapped out the barriers to smooth pastoral transitions. Our goal has been to offer insights into the "dams" or obstacles that congregations face when they seek effective pastoral ministry for their setting. We hope we have identified the majority of tall dams. No pastor or congregation can be alerted ahead of time to all the bumps and barriers they are likely to encounter. All of us who care about congregations must climb in the kayak and make the journey down river.

Appendix 1

U.S. Congregational Life Survey Methodology

More than 500,000 worshipers in about 5,000 congregations across America have participated in the U.S. Congregational Life Survey—making it the largest survey of worshipers ever conducted here. Three types of surveys were administered in each participating congregation: (a) an attendee survey completed by all worshipers age 15 and older who attended worship services during the weekend the survey was given; (b) a congregational profile describing the congregation's facilities, staff, programs, and worship services completed by one person in the congregation; and (c) a leader survey completed by the pastor, priest, minister, rabbi, or other principal leader. Together the information collected provides a unique three-dimensional look at religious life, with results in this book focusing on findings from the leader survey.

First conducted in April 2001, a second wave of the U.S. Congregational Life Survey was conducted in the fall of 2008 and spring of 2009. Both waves included a random sample of congregations that were identified through hypernetwork sampling. Using this method, individuals in a national random sample of adults in the United States who reported that they attended worship at least once in the prior year were asked to name the place where they worshiped. Because the individuals composed a random sample, the congregations they named compose a random sample of congregations. Nominated congregations were verified and then invited to participate in the project. The first sample of congregations (Wave 1) was identified and recruited by the National Opinion Research Center (NORC) at the University of Chicago. The second sample (Wave 2) was identified and recruited by Harris Interactive. Congregations in the national random sample that participated in 2001 were also invited by Harris Interactive to take part in Wave 2.

Of 1,214 congregations nominated and verified in 2001 (Wave 1), 807 agreed to participate (66%), and 434 returned completed surveys from their worshipers at that time (36%). (Congregations that chose not to participate gave a wide variety of reasons.) Of 1,330 new congregations nominated and verified in 2008 (Wave 2), 201 agreed to participate (15%) and 148 returned completed worshiper surveys (74% of those that agreed). Finally, 411 of the 434 congregations that participated in Wave 1 were verified and located in 2008. Of these, 145 agreed to participate in Wave 2 (35%), and 108 returned completed surveys from their worshipers (74% of those that agreed).

In the package sent out to churches participating in Wave 2, we included an eight-page leader survey to be completed by the principal leader in the congregation. The package also included a separate business-reply envelope for leaders to mail back the survey to maintain their confidentiality. Key leaders could also complete the survey online. In addition, Harris Interactive made several attempts by mail and by telephone to contact the principal leader in each congregation that was nominated for the project but declined to participate in the worshiper portion of the study. After several reminders, incentives were offered to remaining nonrespondents to encourage participation.

The leader survey in Wave 1 was funded by the Lilly Endowment, Inc., managed by Dr. Jackson Carroll (Pulpit and Pew, Duke University), and conducted by telephone by NORC. As in Wave 2, efforts were made by NORC to obtain completed leader surveys from congregations that chose not to participate in the in-worship survey. Results are summarized in *God's Potters: Pastoral Leadership and the Shaping of Congregations.*[1]

Our book concentrates primarily on results from principal leaders who participated in Wave 2. A total of 692 leader surveys were completed, which represents a response rate of 39% of the 1,741 congregations nominated and contacted for the project. In our sampling procedures, large congregations were more likely to be identified. To compensate for this size bias, all analyses presented here are weighted by congregational size.

Some analyses include information from the attendee surveys and congregational profiles received from participating congregations. In such cases, only the subset of pastors serving those congregations is included in the analyses.

Finally, many individual congregations and small groups of congregations have taken the survey. Today any congregation can take the survey to learn more about those who worship there and to identify congregational strengths. (See Appendix 2 for details about taking the survey.) Results from these other congregations and samples are not included here.

Additional information about the methods used in this study is available on our Web site: http://www.USCongregations.org.

Appendix 2

The U.S. Congregational Life Survey

A Tool for Discovering Your Congregation's Strengths

Why conduct a survey of your congregation?
- to find out who your worshipers are and what they value
- to consider new missions or programs
- to renew or reevaluate your strategic plan
- to deal with change when your congregation is growing or declining
- to get ready to call a new pastor
- to help a new pastor learn more about the congregation

Who will see our answers?

They are completely confidential; unless you choose to share your results with others, no one outside your congregation will see them. You'll send your surveys directly back to our research office. We'll use an identification number to help us keep track of your congregation's responses, but individual answers are all confidential–in fact, we ask worshipers not to put their names on the survey. We'll combine the responses of all of your worshipers and provide summary reports telling you what they said.

How should we give the survey? We can't afford to mail it to every member.

The survey is designed to be given in worship on a typical Sunday or other day of worship. Giving the survey in worship is an efficient way to take a snapshot of your congregation including regular worshipers, those who come less often, and visitors. If your congregation has more than one weekly service, the survey should be given in each.

Who should participate?

Every worshiper who is at least 15 years old should take part in the survey, including ushers, members of the choir, and others who help lead the service.

How much time will this require?

Most worshipers can complete the survey in 15 minutes. Each question is in a quick response format so that worshipers do not have to write out their answers. We suggest setting aside about 20 minutes to allow time for explaining, distributing, and collecting the surveys.

How can we fit it in our worship service?

Congregations have found a variety of ways to give the survey in worship. Many have found that it works well to set aside the last 20 minutes of each scheduled worship service to distribute the survey. Then worshipers can leave when they have finished. Our experience shows that if you let worshipers take the surveys home with them, few will return them. To make sure your portrait is accurate, it's essential to give the survey during worship.

When should we conduct the survey?

It's your decision when to conduct the survey. Select the week that is most convenient for your congregation. It's best to pick a week that is typical. Giving the survey on Mother's Day or on a holiday weekend, for example, won't give you an accurate portrait if more visitors than normal attend or if many of your frequent attendees are away.

What will we get when we participate?

- Two customized, color reports with detailed profiles of your worshipers (their involvement in the congregation and community, their values, and their hopes for the future) and of your congregation (its unique strengths, especially compared to others of similar size and faith group).
- Two DVDs providing step-by-step instructions for interpreting the reports. They are designed to facilitate group discussion and help leaders identify congregational strengths.
- Two leader's guides with many helpful ideas and tools for making the most of your congregation's reports.
- Two books summarizing the key national findings: *A Field Guide to U.S. Congregations: Who is Going Where and Why* (second edition) and *Beyond the Ordinary: 10 Strengths of U.S. Congregations* (both published by Westminster John Knox).

What will this cost?

The current fees are listed on our Web site at http://www.USCongre gations.org, or you may call 800-728-7228, ext. 2040, to learn more. We'll send you all the surveys you need (forms are available in English, Spanish, and Korean), pens to complete them, and instructions for giving the survey in worship. You'll need to pay for shipping to return the completed surveys to us for processing.

What about other questions we have? How can we sign up?

To obtain general information, visit http://www.uscongregations.org, or if you're ready to get started, please call us toll-free at 1-800-728-7228, ext. 2040.

What is U.S. Congregations?

U.S. Congregations is a religious research group, housed in the offices of the Presbyterian Church (USA) in Louisville, Kentucky, staffed by religious researchers and sociologists who are conducting the U.S. Congregational Life Survey.

Appendix 3

Denominational Families

Catholic Churches:

- Roman Catholic

Mainline Protestant Churches:

- American Baptist Churches USA
- Byzantine Melkit Catholic
- Christian Church (Disciples of Christ)
- Christian Reformed Church in North America
- Eastern Orthodox
- Episcopal Church
- Episcopal/Anglican (unspecified)
- Evangelical Lutheran Church in America
- French Protestant (Huguenot)
- Lutheran (unspecified)
- Methodist (unspecified)
- Metropolitan Community Churches
- Presbyterian (unspecified)
- Presbyterian Church (USA)
- Reformed Church in America
- Russian Orthodox Church
- Serbian Eastern Orthodox Church in the USA and Canada
- Unitarian Universalist Association
- United Church of Christ
- United Methodist Church

Conservative Protestant Churches:

- Advent Christian General Conference
- African Methodist Episcopal Church
- American Missionary Fellowship
- Assemblies of God
- Baptist (unspecified)
- Berean Fundamental Church
- Calvary Chapel

- Calvary Ministries International
- Central Baptist Association
- Christian and Missionary Alliances
- Christian Churches and Churches of Christ
- Church of God (Anderson, Indiana)
- Church of God (Cleveland, Tennessee)
- Church of God of Prophecy
- Church of the Nazarene
- Church of the United Brethren in Christ
- Churches of Christ
- Conservative Baptist Association of America
- Cooperative Baptist Fellowship
- Evangelical Covenant Church
- Evangelical Free Church of America
- Evangelical Friends International
- Evangelical Presbyterian Church
- Foursquare Gospel
- Free Methodist Church of North America
- Free Will Baptist
- General Association of Regular Baptist Church
- Independent Assemblies of God, International
- Lutheran Church, Missouri Synod
- Mennonite (unspecified)
- Mennonite Church
- National Association of Congregational Christian Churches
- National Baptist Convention, USA
- National Missionary Baptist Convention
- Nondenominational
- Nondenominational Evangelical
- Pentecostal (unspecified)
- Presbyterian Church in America
- Seventh-day Adventist
- Southern Baptist Convention
- Vineyard
- Wesleyan Church
- Wisconsin Evangelical Lutheran Synod

Other Congregations:

- Centers for Spiritual Living
- Latter-day Saints
- Reform Judaism
- Reorganized Church of Jesus Christ of Latter-day Saints
- Unity School of Christianity

Appendix 4

Supplementary Information

Figures presented here provide additional information not shown in the figures in each chapter. The figure numbers shown here correspond to the figure numbers in the text. For example, Figure 2.2 here shows the full set of responses that were summarized in Figure 2.2 in Chapter 2.

Figure 2.2: Marital status of pastors by denominational tradition

	All pastors (%)	Catholic (%)	Mainline Protestant (%)	Conservative Protestant (%)
Married	*81*	–	*83*	*97*
In first marriage	65	–	62	85
Remarried after divorce	15	–	20	10
Remarried after death of spouse	1	–	1	2
Not currently married	*19*	*100*	*17*	*4*
Divorced or separated	6	–	9	2
Widowed	–	1	*	–
In a committed relationship	3	–	4	2
Never married	10	98	4	–

* = less than 0.5%; rounds to zero.

Figure 2.5: Highest level of theological education by faith tradition

	All pastors (%)	Catholic (%)	Mainline Protestant (%)	Conservative Protestant (%)
Master of Divinity*	58	48	78	28
Other masters**	10	35	4	12
Doctorate***	15	11	16	13
Total with advanced degree	*83*	*94*	*98*	*53*
Certificate****	6	2	2	12
Bible college degree	8	–	–	25
Total with certificate or Bible college degree	*14*	*2*	*2*	*37*
No theological education	3	1	1	9

*Master of Divinity (M.Div.) or Bachelor of Divinity.
**Other masters includes M.A., S.T.M., Th.M., or other master's degree.
***Doctorate includes Doctor of Ministry degree, Ph.D. or Th.D.
****Certificate from denominational training program, Bible college, or seminary.

Figure 2.8: Housing provisions: Pastors with a manse or housing allowance

	All pastors (%)	Catholic (%)	Mainline Protestant (%)	Conservative Protestant (%)
Manse	38	94	40	26
Allowance	62	30	65	61
Neither	9	2	3	20

Note. Percentages add to more than 100% because some pastors receive both housing and a housing allowance.

Figure 2.9: Health insurance provided by congregation or denomination for pastor, spouse, and children

Health insurance for	All pastors (%)	Catholic (%)	Mainline Protestant (%)	Conservative Protestant (%)
Pastor	71	96	78	54
Spouse (if married)	48	–	55	41
Children (if applicable)	56	–	64	52

Note: – = zero (no cases in this category).

Figure 2.10: Monthly payments toward educational debt

	All pastors (%)	Catholic (%)	Mainline Protestant (%)	Conservative Protestant (%)
No debt	73	74	67	82
Debt, but not currently making payments	14	23	13	14
Debt and currently making payments	13	3	20	4
Median monthly payment	*$324*	*$140*	*$331*	*$169*

Figure 3.2: Small, midsize, and large congregations

	All congregations (%)*	Catholic (%)	Mainline Protestant (%)	Conservative Protestant (%)
Small (1 to 99 in average worship attendance)	48	—	55	56
Midsize (100 to 300 in average worship attendance)	36	24	38	37
Large (more than 300 in average worship attendance)	16	76	7	8

*Note: Percentages do not include a small number of congregations from "other" faith traditions.
– = zero (no cases in this category).

Figure 3.3: Numerically growing, stable, and declining congregations*

In the past five years, the congregation has experienced				
	All	**Catholic (%)**	**Mainline Protestant (%)**	**Conservative Protestant (%)**
Increasing worship attendance	23	23	25	18
Stable worship attendance	27	35	25	28
Declining worship attendance	50	42	50	54

*Growth or decline was measured as follows: Average worship attendance reported in 2008 minus average worship attendance reported in 2003, the difference divided by 2003 average attendance. Congregations growing more than 5% between 2003 and 2008 were designated as "growing"; congregations experiencing a decline of more than 5% were categorized as "declining"; remaining congregations were placed in the "stable" category.

Figure 3.5. Pastors serving more than one parish and bivocational pastors

	All	**Catholic (%)**	**Mainline Protestant (%)**	**Conservative Protestant (%)**
Serves 2 or more congregations	11	24	12	6
Pastor holds another job:	*18*	*8*	*13*	*19*
A full-time job	9	1	2	15
A part-time job	9	7	11	4

Figure 3.6: Types of communities where pastors serve

Type of community	All	Catholic (%)	Mainline Protestant (%)	Conservative Protestant (%)
Rural area	22	18	19	30
Town or small city (fewer than 250,000 people)	51	39	53	51
Suburbs of a large metropolitan area	14	27	14	12
Large metropolitan area (more than 250,000 people)	12	17	14	7

Figure 3.7: Conflict in the congregation in past two years

	All	Catholic (%)	Mainline Protestant (%)	Conservative Protestant (%)
No conflict that pastor is aware of	22	37	19	24
Some minor conflict	56	48	57	55
Major conflict	9	4	10	7
Major conflict, with leaders or people leaving	14	11	14	15

Figure 7.5: Ministry careers of pastors in growing, stable, and declining churches

	Growing (%)	Stable (%)	Declining (%)
First or second career			
Pastor in second career	36	36	47
Pastor in first career	64	64	53
Ever left parish ministry			
Pastor left parish ministry for a time	8	20	17
Pastor always in parish ministry	92	80	83

Notes

Preface

[1] Qualitative studies have made significant contributions to our understanding of congregational dynamics. For example, James Hopewell's classic study, *Congregation: Stories and Structures* (Philadelphia: Fortress Press, 1987), considers three congregations in detail. R. Stephen Warner tracks resurgent evangelism in California between 1959 and 1982 in *New Wine in Old Wineskins: Evangelicals and Liberals in a Small-Town Church* (Berkley: University of California Press, 1988). Nancy T. Ammerman describes field studies of 23 congregations facing community change in *Congregation and Community* (New Brunswick, N.J.: Rutgers University Press, 2001). In *The Practicing Congregation* (Herndon, Va.: Alban Institute, 2004), Diana Butler Bass identifies 50 historic mainline churches that experienced renewal through intentional Christian practices. Ram A. Cnaan et al. documented the church-based provision of social services by Philadelphia congregations in *The Other Philadelphia Story: How Local Congregations Support Quality of Life in Urban America* (Philadelphia: University of Philadelphia Press, 2006). Another excellent example comes from Penny Becker Edgell in *Congregations in Conflict: Cultural Models of Local Religious Life* (New York: Cambridge University Press, 1999). In well-documented case studies of 23 congregations, she examines how conflict affects church life.

[2] Our research builds on earlier work documented in Jackson W. Carroll's *God's Potters: Pastoral Leadership and the Shaping of Congregations* (Grand Rapids, Mich.: Eerdmans, 2006). In 2001, a *Pulpit & Pew* study featured interviews with 883 senior or solo pastoral leaders in more than 81 denominations and faith traditions, making it the most representative clergy sample to date. In addition, data were collected from worshipers in participating pastors' congregations in cooperation with the U.S. Congregational Life Survey. Two other major research projects with data from national random samples of congregations are worth noting. In both instances, insights come from a key informant in each participating congregation without corresponding input from worshipers. The National Congregations Study (NCS), conducted in two waves (1998, 2006–2007) by Mark Chaves (originally at the University of Arizona, now at Duke University), made it possible to gain significant insights about U.S. congregations for the first time, including member distribution, the features of worship services, links between local churches and their denominations, levels of community involvement, and the impact of size and polity. Mark Chaves summarized the study findings in *Congregations in America* (Cambridge: Harvard University Press, 2004) and *American Religion: Contemporary Trends* (Princeton: Princeton University Press, 2011). A third comprehensive national study is the Faith Communities Today project coordinated through the Cooperative Congregational Studies Partnership, representing more than 25 faith groups. Directed by David Roozen of the Hartford Institute of Religion Research, the first benchmark study was conducted in 2000, followed by additional studies in 2005, 2008, and 2010. Release of research reports is ongoing (http://faithcommunitiestoday.org/research-projects-findings). Neither the NCS nor the Faith Communities Today surveys focus extensively on pastoral leadership.

[3] *Beyond the Ordinary: Ten Strengths of U.S. Congregations* (Louisville, Ky.: Westminster John Knox, 2004).

[4] All three books were published by Westminster John Knox in 2002 (2d ed., 2010), 2004, and 2008, respectively. See our project Web site: http://www.USCongregations.org; blog: http://presbyterian.typepad.com/beyondordinary; Twitter: Twitter.com/uscls; and Facebook: search for "U.S. Congregational Life Survey."

146

Chapter 1

[1] The congregational stories in each chapter are drawn from the experiences of a large number of churches and parishes. Although all are based on actual churches, no story reflects the experience of just one congregation.

[2] Herb Miller created the list of challenges to effective leadership in *Leadership Is the Key: Unlocking Your Effectiveness in Ministry* (Nashville, Tenn.: Abingdon Press, 1997). We have updated and expanded his original version.

[3] Barry A. Kosmin, Egon Mayer, and Ariela Keysar, "American Religious Identification Survey 2001," Graduate Center of the City University of New York, http://commons.trincoll .edu/aris/surveys/aris-2001/; Barry A. Kosmin and Ariela Keysar, "American Religious Identification Survey 2008," Trinity College of Hartford Connecticut, http://b27.cc.trincoll.edu/ mt/mt-search.cgi?search=religious+switching&IncludeBlogs=14&limit=20; Michael Hout, Andrew Greeley, and Melissa J. Wilde, "The Demographic Imperative in Religious Change in the United States," *American Journal of Sociology* 107 (2001): 468–500.

[4] Cynthia Woolever and Deborah Bruce, *A Field Guide to U.S. Congregations*, 2d ed. (Louisville, Ky.: Westminster John Knox, 2010), 59.

[5] Ibid.

[6] Ibid., 102–3.

[7] Ibid., 52.

[8] Wade Clark Roof, "Book Review Essay: The Pluralist Ideal in American Religion: The Debate Continues," *The Annals of the American Academy of Political and Social Sciences* 612, no. 1 (July 2007): 240–52.

[9] Woolever and Bruce, *Field Guide*, 92.

[10] Ibid., 93.

[11] Ibid.

[12] Ibid.

[13] "Baptism, Eucharist and Ministry," Faith and Order Paper No. 111, World Council of Churches, Geneva, 1982, 25, http://www.oikoumene.org/fileadmin/files/wcc-main/ documents/p2/FO1982_111_en.pdf.

[14] Jackson W. Carroll, *God's Potters: Pastoral Leadership and the Shaping of Congregations* (Grand Rapids, Mich.: Eerdmans, 2006); and E. Brooks Holifield, *God's Ambassadors: A History of the Christian Clergy in America* (Grand Rapids, Mich.: Eerdmans, 2007).

[15] Woolever and Bruce, *Field Guide*, 90.

[16] Carroll, *God's Potters*, 19.

[17] Anne Dilenschneider, "Soul Care and the Roots of Clergy Burnout," *The Huffington Post*, August 13, 2010, http://www.huffingtonpost.com/anne-dilenschneider/soul-care-and -the-roots-o_b_680925.html.

[18] Mark Chaves, "The Decline of American Religion?" Guiding Paper Series, Association of Religion Data Archives, http://www.thearda.com/rrh/papers/guidingpapers/Chaves.asp; Woolever and Bruce, *Field Guide*, 136. In addition, David A. Roozen, "A Decade of Change in American Congregations, 2000–2010," Faith Communities Today, http://faithcommu- nitiestoday.org/sites/faithcommunitiestoday.org/files/Decade%20of%20Change%20Final _0.pdf, reported one in four churches now has fewer than 50 worshipers.

[19] Ann A. Michel, "Lay Staff Ministry in the United Methodist Church," Lewis Center for Church Leadership, Wesley Theological Seminary, 2011, http://www.churchleadership .com//pdfs/LayStaff_2011Report.pdf.

[20] Woolever and Bruce, *Field Guide*, 113; Roozen, "A Decade of Change" reported an accelerated rate of decline in the financial health of congregations.

[21] Carroll, *God's Potters*, 165.

[22] Rae Jean Proeschold-Bell and Sara H. LeGrand, "High Rates of Obesity and Chronic Disease among United Methodist Clergy," *Obesity* 18, no. 9 (2010): 1867–70.

[23] Woolever and Bruce, *Field Guide*, 117.

[24] Ibid., 18.

[25] George W. Bullard, Jr., *Pursuing the Full Kingdom Potential of Your Congregation* (St. Louis, Mo.: Chalice Press, 2005); Edward H. Hammett with James R. Pierce, *Reaching People under 40 while Keeping People over 60* (St. Louis, Mo.: Chalice Press, 2007); Gary L. McIntosh, *One Church, Four Generations* (Grand Rapids, Mich.: Baker, 2002); Cynthia Woolever and Deborah Bruce, *Places of Promise* (Louisville, Ky.: Westminster John Knox, 2008).

²⁶· Daniel O. Aleshire, *Earthen Vessels: Hopeful Reflections on the Work and Future of Theological Schools* (Grand Rapids, Mich.: Eerdmans, 2008), xi.

Chapter 2

¹· E. Brooks Holifield, *God's Ambassadors: A History of the Christian Clergy in America* (Grand Rapids, Mich.: Eerdmans, 2007), 9.

²· In our analyses, we use the faith group categories generally followed in the social sciences. (Appendix 3 lists all denominations with which participating pastors are affiliated.) The three broad faith groups included here are Catholic parishes, conservative Protestant churches, and mainline Protestant churches.

³· Women serve as pastors in some conservative Protestant denominations, but given the small numbers, none were included in our sample.

⁴· Jackson W. Carroll, *God's Potters: Pastoral Leadership and the Shaping of Congregations* (Grand Rapids, Mich.: Eerdmans, 2006), 72.

⁵· Ibid.

⁶· Ellis L. Larsen, "A Profile of Contemporary Seminarians Revisited," *Theological Education*, 31 (Supplement), 9–11. Barbara Wheeler, Sharon Miller, and Daniel Aleshire, "How Are We Doing? The Effectiveness of Theological Schools as Measured by the Vocations and Views of Graduates," *Auburn Studies* 13 (December 2007): 14.

⁷· Wheeler, Miller, and Aleshire, 25.

⁸· The Association of Theological Schools in the United States and Canada (http://www.ats.edu); Jackson W. Carroll, Barbara G. Wheeler, Daniel O. Aleshire, and Penny Long Marler, *Being There: Culture and Formation in Two Theological Schools* (New York: Oxford University, 1997).

⁹· A small percentage of pastors report they are currently attending a seminary or theological school. In almost all cases, they are pursuing a masters or doctoral degree (2% of Catholic priests are currently attending, compared to 6% of mainline Protestant pastors and 12% of conservative Protestant pastors).

¹⁰· Carroll, *God's Potters*, 19.

¹¹· We asked pastors if they had to be ordained to hold their current position. Most Catholic priests (97%) and mainline Protestant pastors (89%) said "yes." Two out of three conservative Protestant pastors (67%) said they needed to be ordained to hold their position as pastor.

¹²· We considered a pastor "second-career" if (a) they had worked full-time for three or more years prior to entering ministry and (b) they were not a student during that time.

¹³· For pastors in ministry for fewer than 30 years, Catholic priests report a higher number of ministry positions than Protestant pastors. For pastors in ministry for 30 years or more, Catholic priests and Protestant pastors report about the same number of ministry positions.

¹⁴· The description of the pastor's current position probably reflects theological differences as much as it does the actual number of paid, supervised staff. See Chapter 3 for further details on congregational staffing.

Chapter 3

¹· Tom W. Smith, Peter Marsden, Michael Hout, and Jibum Kim, *General Social Surveys, 1972–2010: Cumulative Codebook* (Chicago: National Opinion Research Center, 2011); United States Census, 2010, http://2010.census.gov/2010census.

²· Mark Chaves, *American Religion: Contemporary Trends* (Princeton: Princeton University Press, 2011), 46–54.

³· In addition to congregations in the three main faith groups, other categories of congregations participated in the study (including Jewish synagogues, Buddhist temples, and other non-Christian faiths). We exclude these other groups from the analyses because of the broad diversity in the beliefs and practices of these congregations as well as their small numbers in the overall sample. A total of 692 leader surveys are included in these analyses (194 Catholic priests, 302 mainline Protestant pastors, and 185 conservative Protestant pastors). These numbers are unweighted. See Appendix 1 for further details about weights used in the sample.

[4.] Eileen W. Lindner, ed., *Yearbook of American & Canadian Churches* (Nashville, Tenn.: Abingdon Press, 2010).

[5.] Statistics reflect annual growth from 2008 to 2009 in Lindner, ed., *Yearbook of American & Canadian Churches*, 12.

[6.] Ibid., 12.

[7.] Ibid., 12.

[8.] Cynthia Woolever and Deborah Bruce, *A Field Guide to U.S. Congregations*, 2d ed. (Louisville, Ky.: Westminster John Knox, 2010), 33.

[9.] Ibid., 24.

[10.] Ibid., 29; Chaves, *American Religion*, 64–68.

[11] Edward Stetzer and Warren Bird, *Viral Churches: Helping Church Planters Become Movement Makers* (San Francisco: Jossey-Bass, 2010), 107.

[12.] David A. Roozen, *American Congregations: 2008* (Hartford, Conn.: Hartford Institute for Religion Research, Faith Communities Today, 2009).

[13.] Woolever and Bruce, *Field Guide*, 93.

[14.] Cynthia Woolever and Deborah Bruce, *Places of Promise* (Louisville, Ky.: Westminster John Knox, 2008), 57.

[15.] Cynthia Woolever and Deborah Bruce, *Beyond the Ordinary* (Louisville, Ky.: Westminster John Knox, 2004).

Chapter 4

[1.] Leslie J. Francis, Keith Wulff, and Mandy Robbins, "The Relationship between Work-related Psychological Health and Psychological Type among Clergy in the Presbyterian Church (USA)," *Journal of Empirical Theology* 21 (2008): 166–82.

[2.] Indices were created for each area and are used in subsequent analyses. Because individual items come from questions with different response scales, z-scores were calculated for each item first, and then the indices were calculated as means across the items in the index. The coefficient alpha measure of reliability for these indices are: satisfaction with ministry, .77; satisfaction with external support, .62; satisfaction with personal life, .78.

[3.] Pastors serving in congregations with an average worship attendance of 100 people or more expressed significantly higher levels of satisfaction with ministry than pastors serving in smaller congregations (fewer than 100 people in worship attendance). There were no differences in satisfaction levels with any other areas we measured by congregational size.

[4.] The three indices are correlated at statistically significant levels of $p < .05$.

[5.] Pastors report spending 12 hours (median) each week on preaching, worship leadership, and sermon preparation. They spend much less time involved in denominational, interdenominational, and interfaith affairs (a median of two hours per week).

[6.] See Paul E. Hopkins, *Pursuing Pastoral Excellence* (Herndon, Va.: Alban Institute, 2011), for his description of behaviors, beliefs, and practices that support long-lasting ministry.

Chapter 5

[1.] Body mass index is calculated as weight in pounds divided by height in inches squared, the result multiplied by 703. Obese = BMI of 30 or higher; overweight = BMI of 25 to 29.9; normal = BMI of 18.5 to 24.9; underweight = BMI of less than 18.5.

[2.] "U.S. Obesity Trends," Centers for Disease Control and Prevention, accessed July 26, 2011, http://www.cdc.gov/obesity/data/trends.html.

[3.] Because these items come from questions with different response scales, z-scores were calculated for each item first and then an overall measure of physical health was calculated as the mean across the items. The coefficient alpha measure of reliability for this index is .80. Some of these items come from the SF-12, a health assessment tool. See J. E. Ware, M. Kosinski, and S. D. Keller, "A 12-Item Short-Form Health Survey: Construction of Scales and Preliminary Tests of Reliability and Validity," *Medical Care* 34, no. 3 (1996): 220–33.

[4.] To be consistent with other measures, z-scores were calculated for each item first and then the overall measure of emotional health was calculated as a mean across the items. Also, the two items that were worded in the opposite direction from the others were reverse-coded for consistency. The coefficient alpha measure of reliability for this index is .81.

[5.] "Stress at Work," Centers for Disease Control and Prevention, DHHS (NIOSH) Publication Number 99-101, 1999, accessed July 26, 2011, http://www.cdc.gov/niosh/docs/99-101.

[6.] Z-scores were calculated for each item first and then the overall measure of job stress was calculated as a mean across the items. The coefficient alpha measure of reliability for this index is .84.

[7.] Z-scores were calculated for each item first and then the overall measure of interference was calculated as a mean across the item. The coefficient alpha measure of reliability for this index is .72.

[8.] A helpful and more complete guide to clergy self-care by Linda R. Wolf Jones is available from the Congregational Resource Guide at http://congregationalresources.org/clergy-self-care.

[9.] "Is the Treatment the Cure? A Study of the Effects of Participation in Pastoral Leader Peer Groups," Austin Presbyterian Seminary, accessed July 19, 2011, http://www.samford.edu/uploadedFiles/RCPE/Content/Is%20the%20Treatment%20the%20Cure.pdf.

[10.] The factors listed as strong predictors in this section and those that follow are the ones that make a statistically significant contribution to a multiple regression using each measure as the dependent variable.

[11.] Peter Salovey, Alexander Rothman, Jerusha Detweiler, and Wayne Steward, "Emotional States and Physical Health," *American Psychologist* 55, no. 1 (January 2000): 110–21.

[12.] Chris M. Wilson and Andrew J. Oswald, "How Does Marriage Affect Physical and Psychological Health? A Survey of the Longitudinal Evidence," IZA Discussion Paper No. 1619, June 2005, accessed July 19, 2011, http://ssrn.com/abstract=735205.

[13.] CREDO programs in the Episcopal Church and the Presbyterian Church (USA); the Center for Spirituality, Theology, and Health at Duke University; and the Church Systems Task Force of the United Methodist Church, among others, have a keen interest in pastors' health.

Chapter 6

[1.] Andrew Greeley made this statement based on General Social Survey data, gathered by the National Opinion Research Center, University of Chicago (http://www.agreeley.com/articles/120507.htm).

[2.] I. Ajzen and M. Fishbein, *Understanding Attitudes and Predicting Social Behavior* (Englewood Cliffs, N.J.: Prentice-Hall, 1980).

[3.] Cognitive dissonance is the discomfort someone feels when trying to hold two conflicting beliefs at the same time. See Leon Festinger, Henry Reicken, and Stanley Schachter, *When Prophecy Fails* (Minneapolis: University of Minnesota Press, 1956).

[4.] Factors that are unrelated to thoughts of leaving: age, gender, marital status, children at home, number of hours worked per week, hours spent in leisure activities, percentage of work hours spent in congregational administration, compensation, BMI, physical health, emotional health, and ministry's interference with private life.

[5.] Leslie J. Francis, Andrew Village, Mandy Robbins, and Keith Wulff, "Work-Related Psychological Health among Clergy Serving in the Presbyterian Church (USA): Testing the Idea of Balanced Affect," *Review of Religious Research* 53, no. 1 (2011): 9–22.

[6.] Similar patterns emerged for other types of career changes.

Chapter 7

[1.] Cynthia Woolever and Deborah Bruce, *A Field Guide to U.S. Congregations*, 2d ed. (Louisville, Ky.: Westminster John Knox, 2010), 33.

[2.] The change in worship attendance was measured by subtracting the reported average worship attendance in 2003 from the reported average worship attendance figure for 2008 then dividing that number by 2003 attendance to calculate the percentage change. Congregations in the growing, stable, and declining categories include only those whose worshipers participated in the U.S. Congregational Life Survey in 2008 or 2009. Not all leaders described in this book were serving such congregations.

[3.] The results reported in this chapter are based on multiple regression analysis. Regression modeling allows us to examine simultaneously the impact of a number of independent variables (predictors) on a dependent variable (in this chapter, church growth). The simultaneous entry of predictors helps us understand how church growth changes when any one of the independent variables is varied, while the values of other independent variables are fixed or held constant.

4. Mark Chaves, *American Religion: Contemporary Trends* (Princeton: Princeton University Press, 2011), 111, 58.

5. L. R. Iannaccone, "Why Strict Churches Are Growing," *American Journal of Sociology* 35 (1994): 1180–211; Michael McBride, "Why Churches Need Free-Riders: Religious Capital Formation and Religious Group Survival," University of California-Irvine, Department of Economics working paper, August 21, 2007, http://www.economics.uci.edu/~mcbride/strict4.pdf.

6. Scott Thumma and Warren Bird, *The Other 80 Percent: Turning Your Church's Spectators into Active Participants* (San Francisco: Jossey-Bass, 2011), 23–34.

7. Iannaccone, "Strict Churches."

8. Ian Markham and Martyn Percy, eds., *Why Liberal Churches Are Growing* (London: T and T Clark International, 2006).

9. Cynthia Woolever and Deborah Bruce, *Places of Promise* (Louisville, Ky.: Westminster John Knox, 2008), 90.

Chapter 8

1. Cynthia Woolever and Deborah Bruce, *Beyond the Ordinary* (Louisville, Ky.: Westminster John Knox, 2004).

2. The results reported in this chapter are based on multiple regression analysis. Regression modeling allows us to examine simultaneously the impact of a number of independent variables (predictors) on a dependent variable (in this chapter, the ten church strengths). The simultaneous entry of predictors helps us understand how congregational strength scores change when any one of the independent variables is varied, while the values of other independent variables are fixed or held constant. The subset of pastors whose worshipers participated in the U.S. Congregational Life Survey is included in analyses in this chapter.

3. We measured time investments by calculating the proportion of time the pastor devotes to each task area, given the total hours spent on congregational work per week. For example, if a pastor reported spending five hours per week visiting members and working an average total of 50 hours per week, 10% of the pastor's time is devoted to visiting members.

4. Woolever and Bruce, *Beyond the Ordinary*, 37–45.

Chapter 9

1. Ken Blanchard and Spencer Johnson, *One Minute Manager* (New York: William Morrow, 1982); Paul Stevens and Phil Collins, *The Equipping Pastor* (Herndon, Va.: Alban Institute, 1993); Bill Hybels, "Finding Your Leadership Style," *Leadership Journal* 19, no. 1 (Winter 1998) 84–89; Robert K. Greenleaf, *The Servant as Leader* (Indianapolis, Ind.: The Greenleaf Center for Servant-Leadership, 1970); Jim M. Kouzes and Barry Z. Posner, *The Leadership Challenge* (San Francisco: Jossey-Bass, 2002); Bernard Bass, *Transformational Leadership: Industrial, Military, and Educational Impact* (Mahwah, N.J.: Erlbaum, 1998).

2. Stephen R. Covey, *The 7 Habits of Highly Effective People* (New York: Free Press, 1989).

3. Michael E. Cafferty, *Management: A Faith-Based Perspective* (Upper Saddle River, N.J.: Pearson, 2012).

4. A transformational leadership index based on pastors' views was calculated as a mean across the eight items. The coefficient alpha measure of reliability for this index is .80.

5. A transformational leadership index based on worshipers' views was calculated as a mean across the eight items. The coefficient alpha measure of reliability for this index is .95.

6. The results reported in this chapter are based on multiple regression analysis or logistic regression analysis. Regression modeling allows us to examine simultaneously the impact of a number of independent variables (predictors) on a dependent variable (in this chapter— the various measures of leadership styles). The simultaneous entry of predictors helps us understand the relationship between leadership styles when any one independent variable is varied, while the values of other independent variables are fixed or held constant.

7. Alice H. Eagly and Blair T. Johnson, "Gender and Leadership Style: A Meta-analysis," *Psychological Bulletin* 108, no. 2 (September 1990): 233–56.

8. "What Is Servant Leadership?" Greenleaf Center for Servant Leadership, accessed September 11, 2011, http://www.greenleaf.org/whatissl.

9. An altruistic servant leadership index based on pastors' views was calculated as a mean across the two items. The coefficient alpha measure of reliability for this index is .64.

10. An altruistic servant leadership index based on worshipers' views was calculated as a mean across the four items. The coefficient alpha measure of reliability for this index is .91.

11. Inspired leadership: "I try to inspire and encourage lay members to make decisions and take actions, although I will take action alone if I believe that is needed." Lay-directed: "Lay leaders come up with most of the initiatives in the congregation, although I try to exert a strong influence on their decisions" or "Lay leaders make most of the decisions about the congregation's direction and programs; my role is to empower them to implement their decisions." Pastor-directed: "I make most of the decisions here; lay members generally follow my lead."

12. Jackson W. Carroll, *God's Potters* (Grand Rapids, Mich.: Eerdmans, 2006).

13. Pastors who use all three styles are those who meet three criteria: (1) score in the upper third of the distribution for transformational leadership (using pastor reports), (2) score in the upper third of the distribution for servant leadership (using pastor reports), and (3) describe themselves as inspirational leaders ("I try to inspire and encourage lay members to make decision and take actions").

14. Jim Kouzes and Barry Posner, "The Best Leaders Are the Best Learners," The Leadership Challenge: Leader Talk, April 17, 2011, http://leadershipchallenge.typepad.com/leadership_challenge/2011/04/the-best-leaders-are-the-best-learners.html.

15. Ibid.

Chapter 10

1. The findings in this chapter are based on analyses of a subset of pastors and congregations–those churches and parishes where the pastor completed a leader survey *and* worshipers completed the in-worship survey.

2. The results reported in this chapter are based on multiple regression analysis. Regression modeling allows us to examine simultaneously the impact of multiple independent variables (predictors) on a dependent variable (in this chapter–the measure of pastor-congregation match). The simultaneous entry of predictors helps us understand the relationship between match perceptions when any one independent variable is varied, while the values of other independent variables are fixed or held constant.

3. The original *Empowering Leadership* strength measure included four items, one of which was the percentage of worshipers who strongly agree that the pastor is a good match for the congregation. Because the four survey items are highly correlated, the three remaining items were used as independent variables in three separate regression analyses. Two of these regression equations yielded statistically significant results and are discussed here. But one item (many worshipers feel the pastor encourages them to find use their gifts to a great extent) was not important for predicting congregational match scores.

4. Dean R. Hoge and Jacqueline E. Wenger, *Pastors in Transition: Why Clergy Leave Local Church Ministry* (Grand Rapids, Mich.: Eerdmans, 2005).

5. Herb Miller, *Church Effectiveness Nugget, Volume 21: How to Maximize Personnel Committee Effectiveness*, The Parish Paper, 2009, http://www.theparishpaper.com/files/resources/Church%20Effectiveness%20Nuggets-%20Volume%2021.pdf.

6. R. Michael and Rebecca Sanders, *The Pastor's Unauthorized Instruction Book: What Every Church Leader Ought to Know* (Nashville, Tenn.: Abingdon Press, 1994).

Chapter 11

1. Penny Edgell Becker, *Congregations in Conflict: Cultural Models of Local Religious Life* (New York: Cambridge University Press, 1999), 225.

2. This insight and series of questions were adapted from Herb Miller, *Leadership Is the Key: Unlocking Your Effectiveness in Ministry* (Nashville, Tenn.: Abingdon Press, 1997).

3. Maureen Dowd, "Decoding the God Complex," *New York Times*, September 28, 2011, http://www.nytimes.com/2011/09/28/opinion/dowd-decoding-the-god-complex.html?nl=todaysheadlines&emc=tha212.

4. Cynthia Woolever and Deborah Bruce, *Places of Promise* (Louisville, Ky.: Westminster John Knox, 2008).

5. Trey Hammond, *Places of Promise Leader Guide*, USCongregations.org, February 2008, http://www.uscongregations.org/pdf/leaderguide.pdf; Woolever and Bruce, *Places of Promise*, 89–95.

6. Pete Didisheim, *Toward a New Balance in the 21st Century: A Citizen's Guide to Dams, Hydropower, and River Restoration in Maine*, Natural Resources Council of Maine, http://www.penobscotriver.org/assets/river_restoration.pdf.

Appendix 1

1. Jackson W. Carroll, *God's Potters: Pastoral Leadership and the Shaping of Congregations* (Grand Rapids, Mich.: Eerdmans, 2006).

Glossary

aggregated responses–Sometimes answers to survey questions completed by individual worshipers are combined to describe the entire congregation. For example, each worshiper indicated whether he or she is "male" or "female." Aggregated responses combine all individual answers for a congregation to describe the congregation's gender ratio: 60% are females; 40% are males.

average–The average is a way to describe a "typical" response. In this book, we use the word *average* to refer to the median (see median and mean).

church growth–We measure church growth as the change in average worship attendance over a five-year period. Growth is calculated as change in reported worship attendance over five years, as a percentage of attendance in the first year. For example, if a church reported average worship attendance of 100 in the first year and 175 in worship five years later, we would calculate the growth as $(175 - 100) / 100 = .75$ or a growth rate of 75%.

church size–We measure church size based on average worship attendance reported on the profile survey. We do not use membership figures because different denominations and faith groups use different methods to count members.

coefficient alpha–Surveys often use multiple questions to measure a single concept (for example, satisfaction with ministry). Researchers use a measure of reliability–the coefficient alpha, also known as Cronbach's alpha–that indicates the extent to which the survey questions that make up an index all measure the same thing. The value of coefficient alpha ranges between zero and one. The closer the value is to one, the more reliable the index as a measurement tool.

dependent variable–In statistical analyses, the dependent variable is the *outcome* that is hypothesized to be caused by another factor (the independent variable). For example, if research shows that income depends on the amount of education an individual has, income is the dependent variable.

faith group/denominational family–We grouped congregations into four categories based on their denominational affiliation: Catholic; mainline

Protestant; conservative Protestant; and other/non-Christian. This typology reflects differences in denominational beliefs and polity and is one typically used in sociological research. Appendix 3 shows the denominations reported by pastors participating in the U.S. Congregational Life Survey, by faith group. Because there are few participating congregations in the other/non-Christian group and they come from a wide variety of faiths, most analyses do not include leaders from these congregations.

hypernetwork sampling–Because no database or list exists that includes all congregations in the United States, we used hypernetwork sampling to identify a random sample of congregations. Hypernetwork sampling is based on the assumption that if people in a random sample name an organization with which they are affiliated, the resulting list of organizations is a random sample. Thus we asked a random sample of adults in the United States to name the congregation where they worshiped in the previous year. Those congregations became the random sample that we invited to participate in the U.S. Congregational Life Survey.

independent variable–In statistical analyses, the independent variable, also called a predictor, is the prior condition or factor that influences the dependent variable. (See dependent variable.) For example, if research shows that income depends on the amount of education an individual has, amount of education is the independent variable.

index–Researchers create an index when they combine the responses from two or more survey questions. The multiple questions are designed to measure the same thing. For example, satisfaction with ministry is an index based on three questions: satisfaction with one's overall effectiveness, satisfaction with one's work in ministry, and satisfaction with relationships with lay leaders in the congregation.

leader survey–One key leader in each congregation completed the leader survey. This was usually the pastor, priest, or rabbi. In the few congregations without a pastor, a key lay leader completed the survey. The leader survey asked about the pastor's personal characteristics, background in ministry, current position and benefits, and experiences in his or her current congregation.

levels of analysis–Survey responses can be analyzed at various levels. If all worshipers in a sample of congregations take a survey, results can be examined first at the individual level to determine how individual worshipers answered the questions. Second, by combining the responses of all worshipers in each congregation (see aggregated responses), results can be examined at the congregational level to describe the congregation as a whole. Finally, responses from all worshipers in all congregations in a particular faith group can be combined to examine results at the faith group level to describe the faith group as a whole.

mean–The mean is a way to summarize what is typical or average. For example, the mean age of five children who are ages 1, 3, 4, 5, and 6 would be calculated as: $(1 + 3 + 4 + 5 + 6)/5 = 3.8$.

median–The median is another way to summarize what is typical or average among a series of responses. The median is the midpoint of a series of numbers arranged in order from low to high. For example, the median age of five children who are ages 1, 3, 4, 5, and 6 would be 4–the middle age in the series. We use the median as a single description of what is typical because this measure is less affected by extreme scores.

multiple regression–Some research questions require a statistical technique that examines the simultaneous impact of several predictors (independent variables) on one dependent variable (the outcome). For example, if we want to assess the impact of gender, age, and years in ministry on satisfaction with ministry, we would use multiple regression to do so. Multiple regression requires that the dependent variable be continuous (rather than categorical). Variables such as age and indices such as satisfaction with ministry are continuous.

percentile–We report a congregation's score on each strength measure as a percentile. The percentile score shows the percentage of all congregations that score lower on that strength. For example, a congregation with a percentile score of 75 on the strength Meaningful Worship has scored above 75% of all congregations.

population–The entire group of interest is the population. In our research, we focus primarily on pastors. Thus the population is all pastors in the United States.

predictors–The variables used to predict the dependent variable in a regression analysis are the predictors (also called independent variables).

profile survey–The profile survey was filled out by one person in each congregation participating in the U.S. Congregational Life Survey. This survey asked about the size, denominational affiliation, programs, finances, and other information about the congregation.

random sample–When it is difficult or too expensive to survey everyone in a population (for example, all pastors in the United States), a random sample is used. When individuals are selected randomly from the population, the results from that random sample approach what we would get by surveying every member of the population.

reliability–An index created by combining a set of questions should consistently measure a single concept. If it does so, the index has high reliability. For example, if an index designed to measure satisfaction with ministry is reliable, then each time a pastor answers the questions in the index, the results should be approximately the same (given no major change in the pastor's ministry situation). Coefficient alpha is a common measure of reliability.

response rate–The percentage of people who complete the survey among those initially invited to participate in a survey is called the response rate or completion rate. For example, if 100 pastors are asked to complete a survey and 75 do, the response rate is 75%.

response scale–The set of possible answers to a survey question makes up the response scale. For example, when asking, "Do you agree or disagree that only followers of Jesus Christ can be saved?" the response scale might include five possible answers: strongly agree, agree, neither agree nor disagree, disagree, and strongly disagree.

reverse coding–When combining responses to survey questions into an index, all items must use response scales that are coded in the same direction. Researchers code or assign a number to each response when combining responses. If some items are coded in the opposite direction, they must be reverse coded before creating the index. For example, one question is answered using the response scale of 1 = strongly agree, 2 = agree, 3 = disagree, and 4 = strongly disagree. The second question uses the response scale of 1 = strongly disagree, 2 = disagree, 3 = agree, and 4 = strongly agree. One of the items must be reverse coded to ensure that the codes for each response are the same. In this case, we might code "strongly agree" as 4, "agree" as 3, and so on for both questions.

sampling bias–A sample is biased if certain individuals in the population were less likely to be included. For example, in a telephone survey, households without a landline are sometimes excluded. Thus the sample is biased in favor of those with landline telephones.

statistical significance–A difference among subgroups that is unlikely to have occurred by chance is considered a statistically significant difference. We report this as a "significant difference (p < .05)." The information in parentheses indicates that there are only five chances in a hundred that a difference of this size could have happened by coincidence.

strength measures–We created ten measures of congregational strengths based on worshipers' experiences and perceptions. See Cynthia Woolever and Deborah Bruce, *Beyond the Ordinary: Ten Strengths of U.S. Congregations* (Louisville, Ky.: Westminster John Knox, 2004). Each strength measure is an index created from responses to several survey questions.

weighting–Despite using a random sample, survey respondents may not be representative of the entire population. Weighting adjusts the data to ensure that the sample more accurately reflects the characteristics of the population from which it was drawn and to which an inference will be made. Weighting does not involve any changes to the actual answers to survey questions. In the case of the U.S. Congregational Life Survey, a random sample of congregations was identified by asking each person in a random sample of the U.S. population where he or she attends worship services. Because so many people attend large churches, the random sample of the population included many people from such churches. Thus the sample of congregations they identified was somewhat biased toward large churches. To compensate for this large church bias, we weight the data. Survey results based on weighted data more accurately reflect the true size distribution of congregations where pastors serve.

worshiper survey–All individuals age 15 and older who attended worship services on the day the U.S. Congregational Life Survey was given in a particular congregation completed a worshiper survey. This survey asked about the worshiper's characteristics, participation in the congregation, personal spirituality, and religious beliefs.

z-score–The z-score is a standardized score that indicates how far one response is from the mean of all responses. When questions are asked using different response scales, the responses must be converted to z-scores before they can be combined into an index.

Additional Resources

Anthony, Michael J., and Mick Boersma. *Moving On—Moving Forward: A Guide for Pastors in Transition.* Grand Rapids, Mich.: Zondervan, 2007.

Bullard, George W., Jr. *Leaving, Staying, and Becoming Well Following a Lose/Leave Conflict in a Congregation.* Atlanta: Chalice Press, 2010. http://columbiapartnership.typepad.com/files/bullard-leaving-staying-becoming-well-following-conflict-5.18.10-edition.pdf.

Callahan, Kennon L. *A New Beginning for Pastors and Congregations: Building an Excellent Match upon Your Shared Strengths.* San Francisco: Jossey-Bass, 1999.

Carroll, Jackson W. *God's Potters: Pastoral Leadership and the Shaping of Congregations.* Grand Rapids, Mich.: Eerdmans, 2006.

Clifton, Donald O., and Paul Nelson. *Soar with Your Strengths: A Simple Yet Revolutionary Philosophy of Business and Management.* New York: Dell, 1992.

Daniels, T. Scott. *The First 100 Days: A Pastor's Guide.* Kansas City: Beacon Hill Press, 2011.

Foose, Dean E. *Searching for a Pastor the Presbyterian Way: A Roadmap for Pastor Nominating Committees.* Louisville, Ky.: Geneva Press, 2000.

George, Bill, Peter Sims, and David Gergen. *True North: Discover Your Authentic Leadership.* San Francisco: Wiley, 2007.

Hodges, Wade. *Before You Go: A Few Sneaky-Good Questions Every Minister Must Answer Before Moving to a New Church.* Seattle: Amazon, 2011.

Holifield, E. Brooks. *God's Ambassadors: A History of the Christian Clergy in America.* Grand Rapids, Mich.: Eerdmans, 2007.

Hopkins, Paul E. *Pursuing Pastoral Excellence* Herndon, Va.: Alban Institute, 2011.

Horner, David. *A Practical Guide for Life and Ministry: Overcoming 7 Challenges Pastors Face.* Grand Rapids, Mich.: Baker Books, 2008.

Ketcham, Bunty, and Celia Allison Hahn. *So You're On the Search Committee.* Herndon, Va.: Alban Institute, 2005.

Mead, Loren B. *A Change of Pastors and How It Affects Change in the Congregation.* Herndon, Va.: Alban Institute, 2005.

Miller, Herb. *Leadership Is the Key: Unlocking Your Effectiveness in Ministry.* Nashville, Tenn.: Abingdon Press, 1997.

Morris, Danny E., and Charles M. Olsen. *Discerning God's Will Together: A Spiritual Practice for the Church.* Herndon, Va.: Alban Institute, 1997.

Nouwen, Henri J. M. *In the Name of Jesus: Reflections on Christian Leadership.* New York: Crossroad Publishing, 1992.

Oaks, Fred. *Welcome, Pastor! Building a Productive Pastor-Congregation Partnership in 40 Days.* Lima, Ohio: Faithwalk Publishing, 2005.

Olsen, Charles M., and Ellen Morseth. *Selecting Church Leaders.* Herndon, Va.: Alban Institute, 2002.

Oswald, Roy M. *New Beginnings: A Pastorate Start-Up Workbook.* Herndon, Va.: Alban Institute, 1989.

Oswald, Roy M., James M. Heath, and Ann W. Heath. *Beginning Ministry Together: The Alban Handbook for Clergy Transitions.* Herndon, Va.: Alban Institute, 2003.

Prime, Derek, Alistair Begg, and Al Mohler. *On Being a Pastor: Understanding Our Calling and Work.* Chicago: Moody, 2006.

Rediger, G. Lloyd. *Clergy Killers: Guidance for Pastors and Congregations under Attack.* Louisville, Ky.: Westminster John Knox, 1997.

————. *Fit to Be a Pastor.* Louisville, Ky.: Westminster John Knox, 1999.

Rendle, Gilbert R. *Leading Change in the Congregation: Spiritual and Organizational Tools for Leaders.* Herndon, Va.: Alban Institute, 1998.

Steinke, Peter L. *Congregational Leadership in Anxious Times: Being Calm and Courageous No Matter What.* Herndon, Va.: Alban Institute, 2006.

Stevens, Paul, and Phil Collins. *The Equipping Pastor.* Herndon, Va.: Alban Institute, 1993.

Sweet, Leonard I. *AquaChurch: Essential Leadership Arts for Piloting Your Church in Today's Fluid Culture.* Loveland, Colo.: Group Publishing, 1999.

Sweetser, Thomas P., and Mary Benet McKinney. *Changing Pastors: A Resource for Pastoral Transitions.* Lanham, Md.: Sheed and Ward, 1998.

Weese, Carolyn, and J. Russell Crabtree. *The Elephant in the Boardroom: Speaking the Unspoken about Pastoral Transitions.* San Francisco: Jossey-Bass, 2004.

Wilson, Scott. *Steering through Chaos: Mapping a Clear Direction for Your Church in the Midst of Transition and Change.* Grand Rapids, Mich.: Zondervan, 2010.

Virkler, Henry A. *Choosing a New Pastor: The Complete Handbook.* Eugene, Oreg.: Wipf and Stock Publishers, 2006.

Vonhof, John. *Pastoral Search: The Alban Guide to Managing the Pastoral Search Process.* Herndon, Va.: Alban Institute, 1999.